Praise for Safe from the Past

"In her book, Patricia challenges the past and defies the odds to make a better life for herself. As an expert in non-traditional families, I was touched by her story. It will serve to inspire children considering a higher education but who are afraid to dream."

— Ron Huxley
Licensed Marriage and Family Therapist, author of
Love and Limits: Achieving a Balance in Parenting

"Patricia Miller Mauro keeps you reading. You won't want to put this book down. Her story is relatable, touches your heart, and is uplifting and inspirational. *Safe from the Past* is for everyone who has ever had a dream and anyone who has goals in life. I will recommend this book to all of my teenage students. I look forward to her next one."

— Randi Becker-O'Moore
Work Experience Teacher Coordinator
Joseph M. Barry Career & Technical Education Center
Westbury, NY

"Mauro's *Safe from the Past* is a very personal story about Mauro's troubled childhood and how she overcame many obstacles to survive and obtain a college education. Her perseverance and strong relationship with God is apparent throughout the book. It is from His strength that she found the courage to carry on, fulfilling her lifelong dreams of a college degree and a career. This is a must-read for any young student who has a difficult time dealing with life's ups and downs. A great read that is inspirational and stays with you; I couldn't put it down."

— BeLinda Nikkel
Principal, Heritage Elementary School
Highland Village, TX

"*Safe from the Past* is a riveting and heartfelt story of the trials and tribulations of a shattered childhood and how unwavering faith, along with courage, can right those wrongs through striving and achieving for a better future. This story is a motivating tour de force about overcoming the illusion of insurmountable barriers to a better life, and it will serve as an inspirational and motivational tale for readers young and old. Having known many with similar stories, I highly recommend this book to them, to serve as a testament that there is a better life out there and that the pathway to those dreams starts with the courage inside their own hearts."

— Ryan W. Patton
Teacher, 8th Grade Science
Stephen F. Austin Middle School, Irving, TX

"This book is a gripping story of a young girl's dream to pursue a college education despite the many obstacles blocking her path. Mauro's perseverance and dedication is a poignant reminder to anyone facing challenges in their own lives; to keep believing in their ability to succeed and that with education, all things are possible."

— Holly Duell
Director of Outreach and Donor Services
Foundation for Appalachian Ohio, Nelsonville, OH

Safe from the Past

Safe from the Past

Patricia Miller Mauro

Safe from the Past

Copyright © 2010 Patricia Miller Mauro

All rights reserved. No part of this publication may be used or reproduced in any manner whatsoever without written permission except in the case of brief quotations embodied in articles and reviews.

Manufactured in the United States of America

For information, please contact:

The P3 Press
16200 North Dallas Parkway, Suite 170
Dallas, Texas 75248

www.thep3press.com
972-248-9500
A New Era in Publishing™

ISBN-13: 978-1-933651-84-2
ISBN-10: 1-933651-84-9
LCCN: 2010908696

Author contact information:
safefromthepast@yahoo.com

*This book is dedicated to my
two beautiful children,
Anthony and Isabella,
and to my loving husband, Tony.*

"When you walk to the edge of all the light you have and take that first step into the darkness of the unknown, you must believe that one of two things will happen: there will be something solid for you to stand upon, or, you will be taught how to fly"

— Excerpt from "Faith"
by Patrick Overton

Table of Contents

Preface . . . . *xi*
Acknowledgments . . . . *xv*
   Leaving Insanity *1*
   Unexpected Refuge *15*
   Math, Geography, Economics and Faith *23*
   Without a Home *35*
   My First Break Alone *51*
   Punctured Peace *59*
   The Call Back *67*
   Pain, Fear, and Loathing *79*
   A Leveraged Skill *89*
   Senior Year *101*
   My Father *111*
   Graduation *123*
   The Big Move *129*
Epilogue *137*
About the Author

Preface

During the summer of 1983, I learned some very important lessons. It was hot outside and I was already tired from the heat and humidity. I was due into work once again. At seventeen, I was to report to the Tuscarawas County Board of Education as a secretarial assistant.

I'd obtained the job through a federally-funded program called the Summer Youth Employment Program or SYEP. The program was meant to offer training and jobs to youths from underprivileged homes.

I had already been working there for two weeks when I found out I would be receiving my first paycheck. I was looking forward to going to work for this reason, but the thought of biking across town to a friend's house so I could hitch a ride with her to the job site left me feeling exhausted. I imagined some of my friends hitching their own rides to the city pool, or to the Dairy Queen, in their bathing suits and plastic sandals. Once again, I would find myself carefully navigating the alleys on a bike — dressed in a skirt, heels, and a blouse with long sleeves and ruffles. I was sure the sweat would show through. Would it be as apparent as my lack of confidence?

That afternoon, that first paycheck I received changed my life. Instead of going straight home, I biked directly to the grocery store, cashed it, and bought as many groceries as I could. I had come away with four bags full. To this day, I remember most of the items in those brown paper bags. Why? Because, on that day, I felt what it was like to earn a living for the very first time. Up until that time, our existence had relied heavily on the handouts and kindness of others. You can't imagine how it felt to fill our empty cupboards with bananas, bread, and soup. To fill our refrigerator with eggs, milk, and other things that would also fill our stomachs until the next paycheck. My mom, my sister, and I were so thrilled with our precious commodities.

When I look back on that summer, I realize that I'd learned something else for the first time. I learned that when I worked hard to achieve something, other people seemed to take notice. When other people noticed my efforts in achieving something important, they almost always joined me in the battle to achieve it. I had somehow stumbled upon a little magic.

How do I know this? Because it happened over and over again. There's a lot of truth in the statement, "God helps those who help themselves." When you try and help yourself, others seem to step up and offer their help too.

On our first day on the job, Ruth—another SYEP recipient—and I had reported to the office, first thing Monday morning. I had showed up in a somewhat faded suit and a cracked pair of heels. Ruth had showed up in a pair of tight jeans, a gray t-shirt, and sneakers. At first, Ruth and I were given the same tasks in the back of the building; cutting flyers and other papers with a huge paper cutter.

From time to time, one of us would be called to the front office where three women worked. They had been there for years and were true employees of the Board of Education. Ultimately, one of them would request that we perform an additional task such as filing some reports or fetching some item for them from the back. Most times, Ruth would accept those tasks with no enthusiasm whatsoever. In fact, she would usually shuffle over almost as if the task being asked was too much for her. When they asked me, they got someone who eagerly performed each task with a smile on her face. Pretty soon I was sitting up front as a secretarial assistant, and Ruth remained in the back, cutting papers. It didn't make me a better person than Ruth. But it did give me the opportunity to list on my résumé the fact that I was a Secretarial Assistant. Paper Cutter would have been a tough skill to sell.

Most of this story revolves around my struggle to make it through college. At the time, I felt this was my only hope of having a "normal" life, so a lot hinged on my achieving that goal. What you will see in this story is that same type of magic—people stepping up and helping me because they saw in me my desire and subsequent hard work to achieve something. I helped me, and so God helped me, too.

It's been a long time since I learned those lessons and fought the good fight. But, every once in a while, I stop when I'm standing in the kitchen and take stock of the cupboards that are filled with every conceivable necessity, and then I remember. I remember back to the days when I was "hungry."

If you are ever afraid of doing something because you don't think you can do it, think of this: if it's a true and noble desire in your heart, and you do everything in your power to achieve the unachievable, people will stop and take notice. In a lot of cases, they will even help you. But you must have hope; you must have faith and you must have determination. The rest is magic.

Acknowledgments

I would like to thank The P3 Press at Brown Books Publishing Group. Cynthia, you gave my story a voice. Thanks to Denver Butson who sat with me for countless days in a little Greenwich Village café, poring over the words to this story. Your valuable advice, "You need to show it, not tell it," still reverberates. I would also like to thank a very special group of friends and family who offered their words of support and who encouraged me all along the way. With their help, I have achieved the unachievable. Above all, I thank the One who is behind this story. Thank You for using me to share Your message of hope and faith.

Leaving Insanity

I sat quietly in the backseat while my stepfather drove the car. My mother said nothing as we rambled south along I-77 to Muskingum College, my soon-to-be new home. I could scarcely breathe as I wondered where this road would lead me. I looked down at the only familiar thing—the potted violet plant with its little green leaves, shivering like I was now. It sat in my lap and I grasped onto it with all my might. I pulled up the collar of my mom's coat around me. It was the only other familiar thing I would take with me. She had given me the coat, thinking I could use it since Bill had already bought her a leather one for her birthday. It was the coat that my mom used to wear in more humble times. It wasn't cold outside, but the chill in the car was unmistakable.

During the hour drive there, I looked out across the fogged hills of Denison then Uhrichsville, thinking of what my life had been like, up until now. For forever, it seemed like I could count on nothing, and today was no different. I missed my sister already. She couldn't come that day, because she had to serve hungry customers hot dogs and French fries. We had said our good-byes the night before as we both cried. "Oh, Patti, I'll miss you," she had told me. Like so many times before, I cradled her head in my arms and sheltered her eyes from reality as tears overcame both of us.

"I don't know what I'm going to do now," she said, her voice seeping with desperation. "What if I need to get in touch with you right away? Will you come back soon? When am I going to see you next?" Her questions would have continued, but her voice wouldn't let them.

She was the only person in my life who had traveled this awful road with me thus far, and now we had to say good-bye. When would I see her next? Would she be OK while I was gone? Oh, I had hoped so. I wouldn't be there anymore to protect her. What would happen to her now in that awful house?

I thought back to all the rough times we had been through. From the time we were toddlers, we met a world that was unwelcome and uncertain. My father and mother divorced when we were young. Up until that time, each night had been met with screaming between the two of them as my sister and I lay in our beds in the next room. I would often hold my breath, hoping it would all stop.

My mom and dad were about as different as night and day. Dad had met my mom at Union Hospital. He was a surgical orderly, and she was training to be a nurse's aide. There was something my mom liked about Dad, even though she was already in a serious relationship with someone else. Maybe it was his apparent innocence. He had just arrived in town from Hartville, where he had lived with his Old Order Amish family. He was the second of nine children.

Mom's family lived in town. Mom had already confessed to her mother about her love for her current boyfriend, Walter, but my grandmother did not want to hear any of it. She did not approve of whom Mom was dating whatsoever. When my dad came along and asked Mom out on a date, that was all that my grandma needed. With much force and determination, my grandma was able to convince Dad to present Mom with a ring after only a few months of dating. Soon after, the innocent boy from Hartville and the love-torn girl from Dover were married. One month into their marriage, my mom confessed to my dad that she still loved her ex-boyfriend. Knowing divorce would not be looked upon favorably by his Amish parents, he stayed with her anyway and tried to make the best of things. He didn't want to risk being shunned by his family and religious community back at home.

But, after years of making the best of things, cracks started to appear until a volcano would erupt almost each and every night. It was at this time that my dad decided to file for divorce anyway. In a desperate attempt, he kidnapped his two children one night and took us away from what he would later describe as an unsteady woman — our mother. But my mom fought back, and finally the sheriff came visiting one day and ordered my dad to return us to her. That day stayed in my mind as we lay with her on the couch while she hugged us and cried because she got us back. Kim and I just lay there and rocked back and forth with her arms around us. We felt loved then, but not for long.

Finally, Mom could no longer take the pressures of being a single parent with no money and no higher education. So, we were abandoned and left in the care of one of her "friends" who went by the name of Doris—someone who believed in physical abuse. My sister got the raw end of that deal. From then on, it was a hit with a belt for falling asleep on the couch or a slap across the face if you didn't eat warm applesauce. I tried to console my four-year-old sister as she looked out the window each day and cried for Mom to return, just so that horrible woman wouldn't find another reason to attack. But she always found a good reason to shove us in a closet or to lock us out of the house at night.

During those nights when Kim and I lay on the bed together with the moonlight streaming through the window, I pretended that my dad was looking up at the same moon at the same time. I often wondered why he had not returned. It must have been the phone conversation that my mom had with him an eternity ago that kept him away. She had yelled at him and hung up the phone so hard that it rattled my teeth. I hoped Dad would forgive my mom for yelling and come knocking on Doris's door one day to take me and Kim back to his house. To take care of us like he had before the sheriff had found us. My seven-year-old mind couldn't understand why Mom was staying away, either. Where were they? Why were we here? What would Doris do to us tomorrow?

I tried not to think of my dad too much. I was Daddy's girl and I missed him so much. I pretended he was just away on one of his hunting trips, and he would be back soon. His black- and red-checked jacket would be cold against my cheek when he hugged me after his return. I would tell him he wasn't allowed to hunt ever again, that he had to take us back to his house so we could lie in our own bed at night with the moon streaming through the window and the sound of the clock ticking next to me.

My dad never did show up, but my mom finally came back and retrieved us sometime after my eighth birthday. The pressure for her to do that evidently came from Aunt Betty and Grandma. But there was a problem: she still had no money to support us. So, she applied for welfare and food stamps, and together we moved into an apartment—as strangers but ready to get to know each other again.

In the next several years, we were thoroughly tested. With no job to count on, we continued to exist almost entirely on welfare, food stamps, and the kindness of friends and family. However, that kindness wore off through the years, and we were often left wondering where our next meal would come from or how we could sleep in a room that had no heat as the wind blew mightily outside at forty degrees below zero. A lot of times, we would live in an apartment until we could no longer afford the rent. Then it would be time to move again. I counted the number of places we had stayed during that seven-year stretch. I came up with six places, almost a different place every year. Each place would get worse and worse, too. At the very last place we stayed before Mom met my stepfather, there was a big, brown, dilapidated house on Johnson Avenue. It had no running hot water or heat, and the house smelled like urine, as if someone or something had relieved themselves in the dining room vent. The house was old, and the bathroom that was next to the garage had walls made of Styrofoam. We could smell the gasoline fumes from the toilet.

Then something strange happened, my mom met a man named Bill. He was a tough-looking guy who hailed from New York City. He told her he had moved to Ohio a few years back and was a teacher at the vocational school in the next town. He also owned a hair salon. Many people from the area seemed to know him, and he reveled in this attention. When he met Mom, he found in her someone who was ready to be rescued from her life of poverty. She wasn't bad-looking, either.

Before we knew it, they began making plans for marriage and that's when we all moved into his house on 16th Street. It was a much nicer neighborhood than we ever thought we would belong in. Our life changed drastically, and soon we were living in a ranch-style house that had plush carpet and a dining room that looked privileged and smelled a whole lot better. Almost every night, Bill would cook for us. Dried pork chops taken from Grandma's freezer were replaced with fresh meals of pasta and steak. This seemed too good to be true, and Kim and I slowly settled into this new and unimaginable life.

Then, one night, our reality was shaken again. Like so many nights before, Bill and Mom returned from a party, drunk. It didn't bother me or my sister at first, but we began noticing the same pattern on every weekend. On this particular night, her laughter was replaced with biting words, then fighting. They were horrible drunks, my mom and Bill. This is when we found out that my stepfather hits when he's mad, and my mom hits back when she's drunk. I never knew that about either of them until that time. My sister moved in closer to me and buried her face in my arms and cried, both out of sadness and out of fear. She and I had already gone to bed, but their fighting had woken up both of us. I could hear the fighting escalate, and frenzied footsteps could be heard coming down the hall toward our darkened bedroom. I thought, *Please don't enter our room*. They must have gone into their own bedroom across the hall, and soon we could hear clothes being ripped from the closet. We heard screaming and slapping, and Bill threatening to take his gun out of the closet.

"Oh, Patti!" Kim half-screamed into my sleeve. Her whole body was shaking.

I quickly made the decision to get her and myself out of there fast.

I looked around our darkened prison. My mind was swimming as it tried to think of what we could do to escape.

"Quick!" I whispered to her. "C'mon!" I half-yelled, half-whispered.

I grabbed Kim's arm and pulled her out of bed with me. As she stood there, with the moonlight streaming through the window, I could see her whole body shaking. I had to move fast before our door burst open.

After shimmying up onto the dresser, I steadied my feet, then reached over and carefully opened the window as quietly as I could.

"Pat, what are you doing?" Kim whispered.

I put my finger up to my lips to hush her. I didn't want anyone to catch us. What if Bill and Mom walked in on us, right here and now? What would they do to us then? Would their rage double? Would it suddenly be directed in our way?

I quickly flipped up the screen holders and pushed the screen out. It fell softly on the grass.

I reached for Kim's hand in the moonlit darkness and pulled her up on the dresser next to me. My jewelry box made a slight noise from the force of my heel.

Please God, don't let this start playing music! I silently prayed. God must have heard my prayer, and the music stopped.

I helped Kim closer to the window until she was able to balance one foot on the window ledge.

"Now jump!" I said, my voice harried, as the noise outside our bedroom door was becoming louder and more belligerent.

"What? I can't!" she said.

"Just do it!" I yelled. Had it not been for the screaming in the next room, my mom and stepfather would have surely heard me that time.

Kim turned, brought her other foot up onto the windowsill, then bent over and half-jumped, half-dove, out from our bedroom window. She, too, landed on the soft grass with a thud.

"You bitch!" I heard Bill yell. A slam on our door caused me to lose my breath. What did he do? Had he thrown my mom against our door? I held my breath, thinking that would prevent a gunshot from piercing the air. I thought my heart would beat out of my chest. I had to go right now.

I quickly jumped out of the window, hoping I wouldn't land on my sister. Then, together, still dressed in our nightgowns, we held hands. We snuck out onto the road, and the pebbles hurt my bare feet. We ran down the darkened street, and I wondered where we were going. I noticed the strangeness of how quiet the neighborhood was around us. What a stark difference from the pollution that was spewing from house 131. As we neared the street corner, I heard the creak of someone's front door opening. Bill had noticed us and yelled for us to return. It was the same, rage-filled voice we had listened to just a few minutes ago. We both stopped, and Kim cried some more. I held her close to me, and we shuffled back home to a place that I now feared.

"Where the hell do you think you two are going?" he snarled. He slammed the front screen door hard, and every organ in my body jumped.

Luckily, he did not hit us, but Mom was sporting a nasty bruise on her right cheek.

The next day, Mom had a talk with me. I remember it clearly: she was sitting in her rocking chair with a glass of homemade deep red wine. She was in her nightgown, and it was ten in the morning. She told me that I needed to go to college and asked me what I had planned since I was already a senior in high school. I liked that she wasn't slurring her words yet. It would have made me even angrier.

"Did you apply to those colleges yet?" she asked. She was looking straight at me, and all I could focus on was her blue cheekbone.

"No," I replied. My voice was tired, and I didn't want to talk about school.

"Where is Bill?" I added.

"Out," was all she said. Then she took another drink. I hated the way she drank in the morning. She would cup the glass of wine like a mug of coffee. It was as if she was treating this poison like some precious sustenance.

At least I knew for the time being that I didn't have to retreat to my room. I felt safe for the moment.

One thing that I can say about my mom is that she never gave up on the idea of me going to college and "making something of myself." I would often think, *Are you crazy? Just how am I going to afford THAT when we can't even afford gas in the car?* But I never told her that because she would have disciplined me for being disrespectful. She had always harped on the fact that I would (not might) go to college. She would even tell anyone who would listen, "Pat's going to college in the fall—she's going to become a lawyer or doctor; she's just not sure yet." Even as we had huddled together one glacier cold night with no heat except for the puff of lukewarm air that a space heater provided, she had once again approached the subject of college with me. Whenever I disagreed and told her I'd rather stay back, get a job, and help her with the bills, she would always reply, "No way! I will not have you living this life. You are going to school and making something of yourself, do you hear me? Do you want to end up like me?"

I would look at her like she had ten heads. Was this her way of pretending another event in our lives in the face of impossible odds?

Just like she had back then, she was once again stating the impossible, forcing the issue of college when she knew all along that Bill had clearly stated just the other day, "Don't expect me to fund your schooling—you're on your own when you leave this house." So, there it was—my situation clearly stated by a man who wanted nothing to do with my success in life. My mom wanted it for me, but she had nothing to offer but her own expectation that it *would* happen. Not *might, would* happen.

What was I to do? I definitely wanted to leave this house. That, I knew. I could see that Mom and Bill weren't getting along. Almost every day now, there was a fight of catastrophic proportions that either left the bowl of mashed potatoes from dinner sticking solidly on the wall or an injury for my mother—a fractured wrist, another gift from my stepfather. Both were drinking heavily and constantly. The casual drunk's rule for not drinking until noon was a rule my parents had banished long ago. It was getting to the point where my sister and I were waking up for school in the morning, exhausted and sick with worry. What if Bill ever went through with his threat about the gun while we were at school? Would we come home one day to find my mom with yet another injury? Just how much longer would this madness go on before it all came to one last, horrible event?

Despite my desperate need to leave, I still had the question of where I would get the money to go to school.

I didn't feel smart enough to be a college student. After years of being on welfare, hiding from friends, and the fact that we existed on food stamps and lived in old, pee-infested houses had made my sister and I feel downright unworthy of anything good. In our minds, we already thought of ourselves as lower than all of our other friends. At least I did. College was for those kids who deserved to continue their lives of plenty. They were smarter, richer, and more deserving than I was.

But I needed to leave. My mom was insistent about that, and my relationship with Bill had definitely taken a downturn. We rarely spoke to each other anymore. I couldn't live here much longer. So, I began the huge task of trying to find a college that offered enough financial aid and would at least let me in and cover my expenses for the first year. What I would do after that, I didn't know, but I had to try. I couldn't give up hope, because that is all I had. Little did I know that even though my mother had nothing to offer in terms of financial assistance, she had instilled in me a sense of survival and resourcefulness. I soon realized that these were things that would serve me well in my own fight for survival.

As we turned west on I-70, I steadied my shaking violet. We were on the last leg of my trip to Muskingum.

I felt I was on my way to an entity that was full of other kids who deserved to be there. I had fooled them by being accepted into their institution. They had admitted someone who was undeserving and clueless—someone who used to wash their clothes in the bathtub and who had to boil water for a hot bath. I wondered how long I could keep up the façade. Then I felt an overwhelming sense of sadness—that familiar parting of the ways that you imagine, like the road that splits into two every once in a while in someone's life. I mourned for the loss of my sister and mother. Together, the three of us had forged a bond that now seemed to be breaking, and I felt I was being launched into that familiar dark ocean once again—a place of unknowing. I pulled my mother's coat around me and prayed to God to be with me so I wouldn't be too alone.

Unexpected Refuge

At last we had reached Muskingum College. It was located in a village called New Concord, Ohio. Its population was one thousand when school was not in session and doubled when students were in town. We drove along Main Street, passing a few tiny shops along the way before we reached the center of the street. Our car turned right, and I saw the sign to Muskingum College — "Home of John Glenn." We headed uphill toward a bunch of shady trees. Finally, after some more driving, I could begin to see a building called Montgomery Hall peek from the oak trees. The library appeared suddenly on its left.

I vaguely recalled the layout of the school based on my one trip here from a few months before. I had gone with my stepfather's friend, Billie. I had never met her before, but she agreed to take me to visit and tour the school. My parents didn't have the time, and I guess she felt it was worth it in the name of higher education. I liked her immediately. She was so calm and smart, and she had her doctorate degree.

After a long silence in the car, she said, "If you ever start to think you can't go to school because of a lack of money, don't ever forget that most schools have hidden funds that no one uses, and it's waiting there, just for you."

I thought it was strange that she would tell me that, since anyone on the outside probably would have thought that everything would be paid for me. Why wouldn't they think that? My stepfather owned his own business and had a teaching job. He liked to flash his jewelry and his gold Lincoln all over town. Why would I ever have to worry about money? But I knew I would, because I was arriving here with nothing in my pocket except some old scribbled notes and a fifty-dollar check my mom had written against her and Bill's joint account (without Bill knowing). I kept Billie's bit of advice with me, and it would later pay off.

As we continued driving along the college's main road, my thoughts were jolted back to Mom's comment, "Hmm, this seems like a nice school." Those had been her first words during the entire trip. Bill said nothing. We continued on up a road that passed a sizable lake on the left. At the top of the road was my new home: Finney Hall. After a quick kiss from my mom and a dismissive wave from Bill, I watched as they left, and their gold Lincoln disappeared over the hill. I looked at my bags next to me. Immediately, a residential advisor came outside and helped me with them.

"Welcome!" she said to me. It was the nicest thing anyone had said to me all day.

Trisha was the residential assistant. She was dressed in blue shorts and a peach shirt that didn't match. Her brown hair was flipped up on either side of her head. She smiled at me the whole time.

"You are in room 207. Here is your key. Go on up and get yourself settled. There will be a new student orientation later on in the dorm lobby."

After a few hours of unpacking in my assigned dorm room, I began to wonder when I would meet my new roommate, because she hadn't arrived yet. Her side of the room was still untouched. No clothes hung in the closet, and no sheets yet covered the aqua, vinyl sofa that turned into a bed at night. To bide the time, I decided to call home. From the pay phone in the lobby, I dialed and was met with a terse greeting from Bill. My mom then came on the line.

"Is everything okay, Pat?"

"Yes, everything is okay," I replied, "I guess I just wanted to call . . ." my voice trailed off.

She didn't pry, and I quickly said my good-bye again and hung up the phone. It was strange, this feeling I was having. I felt very alone, like I was missing something, yet thankful, too, because I knew later tonight, voices and fists would once again rise to fight in my mother's house, and I wouldn't be there to listen. I wished my sister was with me so I could hug her and let her face be buried in my arms. I could protect her here. I secretly wished I could have stolen her away to be with me. But I had to let go for now and hope that my sister would continue to endure as we always had together, side by side. Only this time, it would be without me.

As the sun began to sink in the clear sky, I set out across campus. My RA suggested that I should check out the area to get a feel for where things were. To clear my mind, my worries, and my loneliness, I did just that. As I left Finney on foot, another student was unloading her things. Her mom and dad were hugging her, and her mom was crying. Her brothers and sisters were there, too, and they all disappeared into the lobby behind me, their arms around each other in one, big bundle of family.

The first building I wanted to visit was the library. It looked unassuming, hidden among so many trees. You couldn't see it from the main road. As I toured the inside of the building, I immediately liked it. There were students already on the main floor who were either reading periodicals or checking out books. They all seemed quiet and intent on what they were doing, and none of them cared that I had walked through the door even though I didn't deserve to be here. I noticed that to the side there was a staircase leading downstairs, so I followed them. At the bottom of the stairs, I found several tall shelves, filled with stacks and stacks of books. Between each row of books, far back in each corner, was a desk.

I sat at one of them and for the first time, I felt safe from everything as if no one could find me among these trees, down these stairs, between these many stacks and rows of books. No one could find me and start yelling at me because they had too much vodka that night. No one could find me and stash me in a closet and later beat me because I wouldn't eat warm applesauce. All of my past's ghosts were looking for me, and they couldn't find me because I was hidden away among the many issues of *Life* and *Time* magazines. I felt a deep sense of protection in the basement of Muskingum's library. It was a feeling I had never experienced in my life.

This is where I would study from now on. This is where I would hide out from all my memories. This is where I would learn and crank out excellent papers and projects that would get me good grades, a degree, and, one day, a good job. *This is what my mom must have envisioned for me*, I thought as I looked around. I suddenly felt an overwhelming urge to grant her wishes and meet her expectations. "You don't ever want to end up like me," her words reverberated in my mind. "Go make something of yourself." For a split second, I was in awe of my mother. Had she known how protected I would already feel by being here? How was she so sure that I would have a promising future if I came here? After all, I was starting down a path that was never traveled before by anyone in my family. How did she know that at the end of this path would lay a future of financial security? It's not a path she ever took, yet she seemed to know where it could lead.

I remembered how important financial security had become to my mother. Despite her sudden good fortune of marrying my stepfather and no longer having to worry about those endless bills, I had an uneasy feeling that their marriage would not last long. Their heated conversations confirmed my uneasiness. I thought that, before we knew it, Mom might be divorced once again, standing in an endlessly long line, waiting to interview for one job that paid five dollars an hour, just as she had so many desperate times before. She would be faced with angry bill collectors once again, and heat, hot water, and a telephone would no longer be the norm. They would once again become extravagant privileges that she could no longer afford. If they divorced, she would be faced with our old life all over again. And she would be taking my sister with her.

I suddenly realized that I had to do well in school, graduate, and get a job, because I had a feeling that we would soon be poor all over again. Yes, I had to make her proud because I loved her and because she had worked so hard to provide for me and Kim these past seven years, but also because I had to return the favor now and make sure she was provided for in the likely event of a divorce. Hard times were just around the corner—I could feel it. It was a storm whose thunder I couldn't hear, but I could see its jagged streaks of lightning on the horizon. It was coming.

I made a promise to myself right then and there that I was going to do this, despite my own misgivings. I had no right to be here, but I was going to be here and I was going to make it. I knew my first semester was covered, financially speaking. I had enough grant money along with the accounting scholarship I had earned in my senior year at high school. Those two things along with my student loan guaranteed that I was financially covered only during the first half of my freshman year.

Oh, how am I going to pull this off? I wondered. I tried not to look too far into the future and decided to focus on what was more important at the moment: getting good grades and making a respectable grade point average. I figured if I worked hard at being here, maybe someone would take notice at school and work hard at helping me to stay here. It was a ray of hope I had to hang on to that would give me the confidence and motivation to move forward. I couldn't quit—not without trying, at least.

Anyway, what would I have waiting for me if I *did* quit and go back? I would once again be sitting in my darkened bedroom with my sister's tears staining my sleeve, and we would be listening to fights, threats, slammed doors, and Bill spitting the word "gun" in his sentences.

After their divorce, I imagined that the three of us would be back to living our old poverty-stricken life, anxiously awaiting the monthly welfare check at the beginning of each month. I would once again be hiding in the local mart behind the ketchup bottles, waiting for a friend to finish paying for her groceries so I could quickly pay for my own items with those hated food stamps. I would once again share the misfortune of having no food in the house once the food stamps ran out. I didn't want to have to go back to the life of huddling around a space heater for warmth in the winter with blankets that hung at every doorframe to trap the lukewarm air that it provided. I shuddered at the possibility of living through another year of begging for food from my grandma, only to have her give us an old trash bag with freeze-dried pork chops in it for us to eat that she was planning on throwing into the garbage anyway. The only difference was that instead of throwing them into her garbage can, she was giving it to us to consume. Her garbage would once again become our sustenance.

Sitting at my hidden desk in the basement of the library, I realized that I had to go down this untraveled path, no matter where it took me. I had to leave the familiar and search for a future. I could not live in the past anymore. There was no future in the past.

After a few hours, I left the library and noticed that the sun had set. The crickets were chirping like they always did right before fall. I crossed the bridge that spanned the lake and walked uphill toward Finney Hall, noticing how peaceful my surroundings were. I hadn't experienced peace like this in a long time. Usually nighttimes were accompanied by fear and apprehension. After another brief thought of worry about my sister, I walked the last bit toward my dorm room. I wished my sister love as I traveled further along this new path. *I will be back for you and for Mom when I finish,* I thought with a renewed confidence. I hoped they both could hear my thoughts.

Math, Geography, Economics, and Faith

College was turning out to be better than I thought. I was beginning to see just how friendly campus life was. Students would say hi as they walked by, even though I had never met them before. Professors would go out of their way to interact with students on campus. Even the mail clerks gave students their letters and magazines with a smile on their faces.

Despite the friendly and welcoming atmosphere, my mind was still plagued with the worry of how to afford my school books. After all the thinking and planning that went into getting financial assistance for my first semester, I had completely forgotten about how I would afford books. They weren't cheap, either. My book for accounting class alone was eighty dollars. Eighty dollars! That was almost as much as what Mom, Kim, and I used to get in the mail for food stamps for the entire month! Now I was faced with the problem of how to afford five of these eighty dollar books.

Patricia Miller Mauro

I couldn't call Bill or Mom for the money. Bill had made it quite clear that he would in no way be supporting my schooling, and I assumed that included books. I could use the fifty-dollar check Mom had given me, but I was saving that for things like toothpaste and deodorant and it certainly wasn't enough money anyway. I couldn't call Grandma or Grandpa for the money — the most money they had ever given Mom at one time had been twenty dollars.

For a brief moment, I envied my roommate. Her parents sent her a blank check every month for her to fill in and use to buy whatever she needed. I could tell she was well taken care of by the looks of her designer clothes and Estee Lauder perfume. She was one of many students on campus who drove their own car around town. She had no problems affording her books, and I noticed them carelessly stacked on and around her desk in our room. My desk was still empty with only some college-ruled paper and pencils carefully arranged to look like I had more than I did.

I remembered back to when my mom was in a similar situation, years before she had met Bill and remarried. We had no money and no food, and the situation had been getting desperate. We were in the last week-and-a-half of the month — a dreaded time when our food stamps would always run out. Ninety dollars of brightly colored food stamps wasn't enough to buy sustenance for three people, at least not for an entire month. Mom had called Grandma and asked to "borrow" another twenty dollars. Grandma said they didn't have it, but added, "You could come up and take some groceries home if you want. I was just cleaning out the refrigerator." I guess my mom wasn't ready for another portion of half-stale or freezer-burned food and said, "No, thanks."

"But what are we going to do for food?" I half-accusingly asked her.

Freezer-burned food was better than no food. Not only that, Grandma had accidentally thrown in a can of soda in the last garbage bag—maybe she would make the same mistake this time.

Just then, Mom ran out the door and my eyes followed her to a truck that was parked out in the alley. It was a Goshen Dairy truck, and the milkman was making a delivery of fresh eggs and milk to one of our neighbors. I saw her talking with the delivery man for quite a while. He made some more deliveries as my mom stood next to his truck. Finally, after what seemed an eternity, he returned to her and gave her some papers to fill out. She handed them back and suddenly, he disappeared into the truck. He reappeared with milk and eggs and gave them to Mom! Hooray! We would be eating eggs and drinking fresh, cold milk today! Kim and I jumped up and down and ran to the door waiting for our precious food.

"Look what I brought my babies to eat!" she said as she strolled through the door. Her bony hands were grasped around a pint of frosty milk, a pack of shiny cheese, and a box of cereal.

I later found out that Mom had arranged to buy eggs, cheese, milk, and bread from this man using a credit plan where he would deliver food weekly then come to collect the money once a month. Immediately, I questioned where we would be getting this money in a month's time. Mom told me we would cross that bridge when we got to it. My worries were briefly replaced with happiness, and I was reveling in the fact that we had food without the help from the government or from Grandma's refrigerator.

Now, more than two years later, it looked like I was facing a similar situation. *Well, if my mom could figure a way out, so can I,* I thought as I sat in the basement of the library. The next day, I approached the woman at the checkout counter of the college bookstore and asked if they had a credit plan for students where they obtained books and supplies now and paid later.

"Well, yes, we do," she said with a sincere smile. "Will you be using your work-study program funds to pay?"

"Yes," I said, even though I hadn't lined up a job with the college. I further knew that whatever money I did get from a job like that was supposed to be used toward my tuition. The work-study program had actually been built into my tuition payment. Muskingum had already earmarked whatever earnings I would make in a job on campus to help me pay tuition—not books. *Maybe I could work extra hours to pay off any additional costs for books,* I thought. I tried to leave my worries to God.

"Well, go right ahead and pick out what you need from the store and then I'll write up your bill."

I had done it—I had arranged a credit plan just like my mom had. I was going to get my books! *But not so fast,* I told myself. Maybe this woman will find out that

Math, Geography, Economics, and Faith

I hadn't found a campus job yet. I had every intention of getting one and of paying the college back in earnest, but for the moment, I was jobless. *Maybe she'll find me out before I can exit the checkout line,* I worried. I imagined her looking at me in disdain and raising her voice at me in front of the other customers, "Get out of here! How dare you try to get away with this! Go back home—*you don't belong here!*"

I hastily grabbed a basket and filled it with accounting, history, geography, math, and art books. As I headed toward her, I noticed some pens, highlighters, and calculators in my peripheral vision. I grabbed those, too, and with my heart beating so fast I thought it would explode, I reached the counter and set the basket in front of her. One by one, she unloaded each prized item, marking down the item's number and other details on a piece of paper. After what seemed to take forever, she looked up at me, her smile still there, and relayed the total: five hundred and sixty dollars. I signed the paper she had prepared and waited again while she filled three large bags with my books and supplies.

At last, she let me go. I left the store and breathed in a long breath of fresh air. I did it! I couldn't believe it. Somehow I had figured out my first major problem without anyone's help. I happily walked across campus, over the bridge across the lake, and back to my room where I unloaded everything on to my desk. At last, my side of the room was beginning to look like that of a real college student. Later that night, I grabbed a few books and went back to the library basement where I began to study accruals and expenses. Now I could focus on getting some good grades. As for how I would afford my purchase, I decided that I would worry about that later. For now, I had to focus on my studies.

A few weeks later, while sitting with my roommate Holly in the Patton Hall cafeteria at lunchtime, she asked, "Where do you go after dinner?"

I was taken aback by her question. She must have seen my startled look, because she then clarified, "Me and the other girls on the floor were looking for you the other night. We were thinking of going into Zanesville for some shopping at the mall."

My first thought was, *I have no money to shop,* then my second thought was, *How would I find time to study if I left campus to go shopping, even for one night?* The thought of not having the library to go to at night seemed kind of scary. After all, that's where I felt safest.

I told her I was visiting a friend in nearby Kelley Hall. "Oh," was her answer, and I left it at that. Actually, Holly was so far a very sweet roommate. She offered to loan me clothes to wear as she did for all the girls on the floor. Everyone wanted to borrow her designer jeans and polo shirts. She was very generous and even asked me to come home with her one weekend to meet her parents.

As we left the cafeteria, I turned to the coat rack to get my mother's coat. At first glance I couldn't find it.

"I'll see you back in the room," I told Holly as I continued searching for it.

I distinctly remembered hanging it on one of the hooks on the coat rack that sat right outside of the cafeteria

Math, Geography, Economics, and Faith

doors. I knew I had brought it, because it was cold outside. Even the short walk from Finney to Patton Hall required a coat. My search became more and more frantic. This was my mother's coat. I couldn't part with it—I must find it. It was the coat my mom had worn so many times when the three of us lived and suffered together. She had worn it as we all huddled in our Johnson Avenue house. It was what helped to keep her warm from the cold that lingered in the rest of the house. The space heater alone was not enough to warm her—the coat was what helped her to stop shivering. She had given me that coat a week before I left for college. I cherished it, because it was the only thing I still had of hers. Everything she now had was from her new life. When I wore her coat, I felt as if her own arms were hugging me.

I took one more look behind a purple coat with big gold buttons, and there I found it. With great relief, I grabbed onto it and held it to me. I blinked a few times to clear the tears in my eyes. As I started putting it on, I noticed that something didn't seem right. I fanned it out and to my horror, noticed that the coat had been cut lengthwise, several times, as if someone had attacked it with a razor. *Who on earth would do this?* I asked myself, then immediately tears began streaming down my face. I quickly turned away from the cafeteria as other students were leaving. I was shocked. My heart beat faster and faster as I thought, *Just who would do an awful thing like this? What am I to wear now? There is snow outside!*

Just as quickly, I felt as if someone had attacked me and my mom, and I immediately felt such grief. It was the last thing I had of my mom from our old days. It has been a reminder to never give up—to fight against our poverty. And now it was all shredded to pieces, all while I had been eating in the next room.

Questions swirled in my mind. *Who would do this? Why?* I left with my mother's shredded coat cradled in my arms and went back to the dorm room. Thankfully, Holly hadn't yet returned, so I locked the door and placed the coat on my bed. As I stared at it some more, I cried hard. What was I going to do? My mom's coat was ruined. The last piece of her was gone, and all I had left of her old self and our old life were my memories. Just like everything I had held dear, it was ripped to pieces. To further the sting, I had nothing to wear and it was cold outside. What was I going to do?

The only thing I could think to do was to report the incident to the college's student life representative—Dean Anderson. I wasn't sure if this was the proper protocol, but I was going to at least approach him about it. It was a cold walk down the hill, across the lake to the campus. I wore a sweater, but it didn't seem to keep the cold out like my mom's coat could.

Dean Anderson's office was at the top of one of the recreational buildings. In fact, the building was called Top of the Center. I asked his secretary if I could meet and talk with him. She rose from her desk and gestured for me to follow her. I was nervous, because I had never met this man before. What if he was mean and dismissive? What if he could see the type of person he was talking to and order me out? What if he had a conversation with the woman at

Math, Geography, Economics, and Faith

the bookstore? I prayed a silent prayer, *Please don't let this man kick me out of his office. Please, God, give him a listening ear.* I pulled together whatever courage I had and walked into his office. I was met with a very kind-looking man with sandy hair and a brown business suit on.

"Please, have a seat," he asked, and so I did.

I immediately noticed the pictures of his family on his desk. To my left, I could see many degrees lining the wall. Dean Anderson was head of the college, head of the psychology department, and was even one of the psychology professors.

"What can I do for you?" he asked. He smiled just as sincere a smile as the checkout lady in the bookstore.

I proceeded to tell him what had happened to my coat. Of course, I left out any details about its significance. I only wanted him to know the basic details: that I had no coat and that I thought it might have been vandalized.

After he apologized for my inconvenience, he asked, "Have you called your parents so they can send you a new one?"

I hesitated and replied no. A few awkward seconds later, I added, "I can't." Then I averted his gaze, and he said nothing for a long time. I looked down at the floor away from his degrees, his family pictures, and his eyes. *Oh, no,* I thought. *He is sure to find me out now.*

Then the big question came and he asked, "Do you have any money to buy a new coat?"

I shook my head. I couldn't say anything at this point, because my voice surely would have given me away and I would have started crying all over again.

I steadied my voice and asked, "If the college has some sort of emergency fund for things like this, I would gladly pay them back . . . ," then I stopped just short of tears.

After a few seconds, he replied, "Well, the college does happen to have a fund for things like this." His answer caught me off guard, and I looked up at him with renewed hope.

He then reached into his pocket, pulled out his wallet, and produced two fifty-dollar bills. He walked around his desk to where I was sitting and handed them to me. I was thankful for the chair. There was no way I would have found the strength to stand through this conversation.

"Do you have a means to get to the mall?" he added.

I hadn't thought of that yet, but he had a point—just how *was* I going to get to a store to buy a coat? The nearest department store was nineteen miles away.

Without waiting for a reply, he reached into his desk and pulled out a set of keys.

"Here, take my car."

I slowly took the keys from him. I couldn't believe he was offering his very own car so I could buy a coat.

"I'm parked behind Cambridge Hall in the first spot on your left."

I slowly got up out of my chair and walked toward him. An earnest thank you was all I could utter before leaving. I was in shock once again at the kindness of this stranger. He had never met me before, and already he was giving me money and the keys to his own car.

Math, Geography, Economics, and Faith

Didn't he know who I was? Couldn't he tell that I wasn't your normal Muskingum College student? That I really didn't belong here with all of the other designer-wearing students? Somehow, though, in a strange way, I could tell from the look in his eyes that he knew exactly who I was and the type of person he was talking to. And he didn't seem to mind in the very least.

After leaving the building, I allowed myself to finally look up to the overcast sky, and I said, "Thank you." My heart was light, and my mind still couldn't believe what had just happened. Just then, a bird flew very low overhead, and it reminded me of the story at Sunday school in which God said He takes care of the birds without a worry from them. And if He can love and take care of the fowl of the air, then He could certainly love and care for us humans, too. I envied that bird. I wished I could wake up every morning, knowing—not assuming, not wishing, not hoping, not even thinking, but knowing—God was going to take care of me that day. If I could be like that, I would be as light and carefree as a bird. They say that faith can move mountains. I wondered what it would be like to have faith like that. Would I ever know? Does anyone ever know such a faith? For the little faith I did have, there was one thing clear: it was tested often and the next few months would be no exception. But for now, God was taking care of me, and my heart filled with thanks.

Without a Home

It was the latter end of the first semester as I sat in the financial aid office, waiting to speak with the financial aid officer. Mr. Zellers had sent me a note, asking to meet with me. I knew what he wanted to talk about. The second semester was just beyond these next few months, and I had not submitted any sort of payment plan whatsoever to cover it. I eagerly awaited our meeting, hoping he would know better than anyone on this campus what kind of financial assistance I could get. I had high hopes that they would be able to help me in some capacity.

As I waited in his office to see him, my mind wandered to just how much I liked Muskingum. I was feeling more and more at home at college than I had ever felt anywhere else. In fact, I often thought that if I stayed the full four years here, it would be the longest I've ever stayed anywhere in my life. Usually, Mom, my sister, and I had lived in an apartment or rental house for maybe a year or two before moving on. The last place I lived in before school had proven that; I was a resident in Bill's house for approximately six months before moving to school.

College had become home to me in more ways than one. I was beginning to relax and trust my surroundings. I wondered if that's how most people felt at home on a normal day-to-day basis. If so, it was a wonderful feeling. Students and faculty, and even those people who worked in administration, were never short on kindness. Students continued saying hi to you when you crossed their path, and this happened every single day. I had a warm place to sleep and study in my dorm room, and meals could be counted on three times a day, without fail, from the cafeteria.

I didn't have to worry about the college not paying their bills and suddenly closing the cafeteria. Food would always be there. I didn't have to worry about having no heat in the winter. My room was toasty, night after night, and that was without having blankets hang at every door and a space heater. Here at school, everything was paid for and, for a time, I began to relax a little and realize that I didn't have to constantly retreat to the library basement for safety. I began to venture out and explore the other buildings on campus at night during study time.

My thoughts of campus life were snapped back to reality when Mrs. Sayers suddenly popped her beehive-head out into the waiting room and, in a very low but polite tone, told me, "Mr. Zellers will be with you shortly. He just got tied up in a phone call right before you came in."

I smiled back at her and crossed my legs. I looked down and noticed that a hole was forming just outside of my canvas tennis shoe, right where my pinky toe was. I quickly crossed my legs the other way, hoping no one else would see it.

I remembered Mr. Zellers, back when he visited Dover High School. He had come there with a few other representatives from other colleges during the school's college week. He seemed like a nice man at the time, but this would be the first time I would visit with him face-to-face. My admission to college and the financial aspect of my admission had all been handled through the mail until this point. His door was shut, and Mrs. Sayers was typing busily on an automatic typewriter.

I wondered what Mr. Zellers would have to say to me. What if he asked how the second semester would be paid? How could I tell him, "I don't know"? Would he laugh, look at me sternly, or kick me out of school, right then and there? I remembered how he had mentioned how much financial aid the college had available when he visited my high school, and I was counting on that heavily. For some reason, I wasn't worried as much as I thought I would be. I guess I figured that God would provide, and I would have financial aid. I said another quick prayer for help.

As I continued waiting to the click-clack of Mrs. Sayer's typewriter, I let my mind wander again to all the other things I liked about Muskingum. I looked out the window and noticed Cambridge Hall right next door. Cambridge Hall was the accounting, economics, and business law building. It was the building where most of my classes were held.

Cambridge Hall started becoming a favorite of mine. I quickly began making friends with other "regulars" who also chose Cambridge as their study place of choice in the evenings. Along with their friendships, I also found among them students who didn't mind explaining to me the concept of "a curve that increased at a decreasing rate" in economics or some other assignment I had trouble conceptualizing. Often, these older students would happily pull me aside into an empty classroom and use the chalkboard to explain their version of what Keynesian economics was all about or to explain the logic behind cash management accounting. We became such good friends that they often invited me over to their fraternity or sorority to hang out, and sometimes I would take them up on their offer. The best times of all, though, were my walks back to my dorm room at night after I had finished studying.

It was during these times that I felt at peace the most. Usually, the campus was mostly clear of the student population, so on my walk back I encountered only a student or two. The only sounds I could hear were the ripples of the water on the campus lake and the chirpings of crickets in the still, night air. Sometimes I would look around me, almost disbelieving of the stillness that surrounded me. The peace and calm I was experiencing seemed to be so distant from the chaos of the hitting and fighting that was probably going on in my mother's house. I worried about my sister a lot. We promised to write each other but, despite the many letters I sent, I hadn't received a single one from her.

My sister seemed different when I had gone back home for the weekend a few months before. It was as if she was somewhere else, almost distant. I had asked her if everything was okay and she told me that things were the same — maybe even a little worse. Bill had changed, too, and in a way I almost felt like I was staying at a stranger's home. We had been distant with each other ever since he married my mother. With his gregarious nature, he put on a great show for friends and family, but that had been so different from the hotheaded and sometimes moody nature I had seen in him all the other times. I guess I considered him somewhat of a phony. Most of the times I kept to my room, and my weekend away from college was no different. I felt very uncomfortable and longed for the stillness of Muskingum College. I was glad to return a few days later.

Muskingum College was my home now. I was safe and taken care of here. Now, as I approached the new year, I couldn't believe I had made it through the first semester, and with a good grade point average to boot. Mrs. Cheng, my accounting professor, had even complimented me on my good grades, and what was strange was that I didn't have to study all that hard to get them. Half of the material she had tested us on I had already seen on past tests from high school. It hadn't gotten hard yet. Maybe college wasn't off limits to a person like me after all.

I remembered back to my first weeks at college and the struggles that I had endured just to be able to stay in school.

I remembered my first major challenge. On that first Sunday evening right after I moved into college, I was hit with an unexpected reality. I noticed that the doors of the cafeteria were locked and it was dark inside.

"The only time the cafeteria closes during the week is on Sunday nights," Holly, my roommate, had informed me. "It's the one day the staff has off."

I had no idea, and at once I began to wonder where I was going to get Sunday dinner next week and every week after that. At least I had enough of my mom's check money left over for a little pizza tonight. But what was I going to do for all my remaining Sundays?

Then I remembered some of the students talking about working in the cafeteria. They hated it because they said it was an exhausting and dirty job. I figured if I got a job there and made sure I worked on Sunday afternoons, I might have a chance at getting to some of the food back in the kitchen. If I could do that, I might have a source for my Sunday dinners. After all, that's where you worked, back in the kitchen, and this was closer to the food than anywhere else. So, I approached the manager there and he happily agreed to hire me. I was thrilled! On top of that, no student wanted to work the weekends — that was their time. I excitedly snatched all of the weekend slots. I now had potential access to food for Sunday dinners.

I was to find out that it was a tough job, but not as bad as I thought it would be — not if you didn't let it get to you. The job entailed donning an apron and standing behind a steel table with a dug-in trench filled with running water. Cafeteria workers would bring in huge steel carts filled with trays of uneaten or half-eaten food. My job was to unload bowls of Jell-O, cups of soup, half-eaten slices of meatloaf, and warm glasses of milk. I did this with my bare hands, scooping their leftovers so they fell into the running water and down a drain. Once I rinsed the dishes, I would load them onto another tray and slide that down for another person to load into a gigantic dishwasher that puffed out steam from near where I was standing. Pretty soon, I was getting the hang of it and could unload a cart full of fifty trays in only a few minutes. It was a good thing, too, because in my two-hour assignment I unloaded twenty steel carts on a busy day.

After the two hours were over, my apron would be smeared with all kinds of food and my hair would be a matted mess as if I had just taken a shower. I smelled of everyone's lunch, so I always had to follow up work with a shower back at the dorm. But the best part was working on Sunday afternoons. That's when I enacted my plan. The cafeteria was getting ready to close until Monday morning. Right before leaving, just after my shift, I hastily approached the dessert manager and asked her if I could take some baked goods back to my room. "They were so delicious today," I said as I looked over at them standing on their own set of steel carts. They were cooling and I could smell their sweet aroma from the puffing dishwasher.

She said, "Of course, anytime! Take as much as you'd like."

Quickly, I was stuffing brownies, cookies, and banana bread into my coat pockets, as much as they could hold. This would be Sunday dinner.

With that challenge now a memory, I had a new problem. How was I going to be able to afford the upcoming semester?

Suddenly, the familiar click-clack stopped and Mrs. Sayers gestured for me to go on into Mr. Zellers office. As soon as I sat down, he turned to me amid piles of papers stacked high on his desk. He was a thin man and his face was kind and warm. He smiled and introduced himself. After we shook hands and exchanged the usual pleasantries, he asked me if I had lined up the funds for the second semester tuition. I gulped, took a breath, and told him I was working on it.

"Oh — are your parents sending us a check?" he asked, nonchalantly.

"Uh, I don't think so," I replied as fear gripped my heart.

He looked up from his paperwork with a confused look on his face.

"But a friend of mine once told me that colleges always have hidden monies lying around that students can sometimes use to pay for school," I added.

I wasn't sure if I was supposed to say that, but that's what I remembered Billie telling me — the woman who had taken mc on my tour of the campus earlier in the year.

Mr. Zellers looked at me intently and said, "Your parents are not funding you?"

I hesitated for a minute and said, "No."

I figured I didn't have much to lose so I took a deep breath, closed my eyes, and added, "My stepdad and I don't get along and he would never agree to pay for my tuition. Isn't there something else I could do or apply for that would help?" There. It was out in the open now and my words hung in the air like a dark cloud.

I looked down at the floor, embarrassed that he was hearing this. *Not good enough, you're not good enough!* the voice in my head kept repeating. *You don't belong here!*

"Would it help if I contacted your stepdad and had a talk with him? He needs to know that if you don't have the money to pay, you won't be allowed to continue here at Muskingum."

Those words stung so badly—it felt as if someone had plunged a knife into my lung and I gasped. I knew it had always been a fear but now it had been confirmed verbally, in the open, by none other than the financial aid officer himself.

Fighting back tears I said, "Isn't there any financial aid I could get that would help my situation?"

But my tears betrayed me anyway and a few began falling down my cheeks. They stung my hot cheeks and I thought I would dwindle into a puddle of nothingness. My face felt warm and red. I turned toward the window. Shame enveloped me.

Oh, why do I have to be like this? Why can't I be like other kids who didn't ever give college a second thought? Coming back was a given for them. But oh, no, not for me!* My feelings of embarrassment were mixed with anger.

I could see that he felt surprised at what I said and how I reacted because after that it seemed like an eternity before he began speaking again, and when he did, he seemed to choose his words very carefully. I was glad. I couldn't bear one more stinging word.

With that, he picked up the phone and began dialing what I recognized as my home phone number. *Oh, no,* I thought. He was going to talk to Bill. *This is not good.*

Someone picked up because I could hear Mr. Zellers's side of the conversation. "Hello, Mr. Levenger?" I heard him say.

I quickly got up and left his office, pacing back and forth in front of his door. I couldn't bear to hear what my stepdad was sure to tell him. I imagined Bill yelling into the phone, "Well, I'm not paying! I told her that! Didn't she get the message? Who does she think she is and what does she think she's pulling here?"

It was during these times that I couldn't even remember to pray. I couldn't think past my sheer fear and panic. I tried to remind myself to pray during the worst of times, but already I had forgotten.

After a very long time, I could hear the phone hanging up, and I slowly walked back into his office. I looked at Mr. Zellers with some false hope, but right away I knew. His eyebrows were crinkled as if angry but he talked to me in a gentler voice than before.

He said, "I can't believe your family won't help you out." He shook his head and looked across all the deep piles of paper as if something would jump up with an answer. He knew what my stepfather made in a year—it was all included in the application. I guess it didn't make much sense to him.

"Well, I do have something you might be able to apply for," he slowly stated as he sifted through a stack of paperwork. "It's called the Henry Strong Loan. Not many students even know it's there and, to date, we've only had three other students use it."

Billie was right! There were funds that every school had that were just laying around, waiting to be used, that is, if you discovered their existence. I wondered why these monies were such a secret.

"But you'll only be able to use it for the next few semesters. There is a limit to the amount of money you can take for tuition and we'll have to spread it out so we can make sure you keep coming here."

I could have cried tears of happiness right there in his office. But at that moment, I felt a mix of extreme anxiety, anger at Bill, and thankfulness that God had helped me discover another way out once again.

Then Mr. Zellers asked me a question I wasn't expecting: "Are you on your own now that you're in school?"

I nodded my head to confirm that I was. I wondered why he had asked me that.

"Patti, here's what I need you to do. The law states that if you live independently from your parents for two years after you leave home, you can claim a status of independent. If you are financially independent, your financial aid will be based on your income and not on your family's income. But that means your stepdad can't claim you on his income tax returns for these two years, either. It might mean a couple of rough semesters here at Muskingum, financially speaking, for now. But I might be able to get you the assistance you need for the first two years if you can work on getting this status. Do you think you can get your stepfather to work with you on this?"

He added, "If you can do this, your last few years at Muskingum will be a lot easier. You have to try to get this done. If you don't, I'm not sure you'll be able to continue here."

"I don't know, but I'll definitely try," I replied, hopeful that this could be my one chance to at last afford school for the last two years of college.

Oh, how nice it would be not to worry semester-to-semester about where I was going to get the money to pay for school. If I could get Bill to do this, then I could be home free, financially speaking, for my junior and senior years of college.

I was resolved to speaking with Bill and laying it out on the line with him. I needed to have him agree to this. *Maybe he will*, I thought. After all, I wasn't really living at home anymore. What need would he have to keep me on his tax returns? We were barely on speaking terms with each other, just because we had nothing really to say to each other, but maybe he would be willing to hear me out. I had to give it a try. It was my only hope for staying in college and getting a degree. I just couldn't bear the thought of leaving school, my Cambridge Hall friends, the still nights across the lake, and the protective library walls.

After my meeting with Mr. Zellers, I signed up for the Henry Strong Loan and secured my spot in the class of 1988 for one more semester. After that, I called Mom and told her about my conversation with the financial aid officer. I was afraid to speak to Bill directly. Mom promised to speak to Bill and said she would call me back with his response.

A few weeks later, Mom contacted me and told me Bill had agreed to remove me as a dependent on his taxes on one condition: that I was never to return home again.

"What do you mean?" I asked angrily. I couldn't believe what she was saying. "I don't live at home anymore, remember?"

"No, Pat. He means you are not allowed to come home during school breaks either."

"What? Is he joking?" I asked her.

My mom replied, "I talked to him for hours and hours about this. You don't understand how much I want you to come home, honey, but you know how it is here. He is a stubborn man..."

I slammed the phone back down on the receiver. How dare she accept this ridiculous suggestion. I couldn't believe I was being kicked out of the family! I was around before he even came onto the scene, now he was calling the shots and redefining who our family would be. Why was Mom going along with all of this?

I ran back to my dorm room and slammed the door. Hot tears stained my face once again and I hated Bill for the person he was to me. How dare he treat me like this! He was practically kicking me out of my own family. What was I going to do during school breaks? Would I ever see my sister again? How could he do this to me and how could my own mother let this happen? I hated him with every ounce of energy I had left. My legs felt like liquid, and I hastily sat down and began to cry harder.

Where are You now God? Why do You allow people to treat others like this? Why aren't You here? Why can't I have a real dad who would actually care for me or at least hug me for a half second? Why does my roommate get to have caring parents who send her weekly checks in the mail? Why can't I have a family like any other student on this campus? Why does it have to be so different for me? Why me? Where are You? Are You even there?

I cried harder than I had in a long time. I was so mad at my stepfather and my mother, and now I was thinking things about God that I would never think of saying. How could I think these things when He had helped me so many times before? Could I ever be forgiven for such things?

A few hours later, exhausted from all of the mixed feelings I was having, I resolved to accept this part of my life and to move on. I had to. What other choice did I now have? What made things worse was, if I failed at college now, I would have no place to go home. I would be back in my mother's previous position of looking for a job, not getting one, and being on welfare. Only this time I would be alone.

I just had to make this work and prove to Bill, my mom, and Mr. Zellers that I could do it. I suddenly became more determined than ever to make things right for myself. I was going to finish college, graduate, and make something of my life and nothing was going to stop me. One day I would say good-bye to all of the hurt and pain my life was infused with. One day, I would experience peace.

My thoughts quickly switched back to my current worries. Spring break was starting in the next few months. *How was I going to eat when the cafeteria would be closed every single day? Would they even let me stay in a dorm that will be emptied of students by noon on Friday? If I stayed on campus, who would I talk to if everyone went home? What would I do for money?* These questions swirled around in my head until I fell asleep in a haze of exhaustion.

My First Break Alone

My fear of spring break became a reality in the month of March. I shuddered at the thought of being the only person left in my three-story dorm building. What would the campus be like without any students? How was I going to eat these next seven days with no money? Christmas break had been easy. Holly had been nice enough to take me home with her and I spent the holidays with her and her parents. But this time around, she excitedly informed me that she was to spend spring break in Florida. I wished her a fun vacation, but in the back of my mind, worries loomed like that all-too-familiar thunderstorm.

It wasn't just a simple problem of not eating on Sunday evening anymore. This was going to be a huge dilemma if I couldn't get food for breakfast, lunch, or dinner each and every day. I had absolutely no money left. It had all gone to toothpaste, deodorant, and stamps—all the necessary things that kept me just above water that first semester. Now I didn't have a cent to my name and, once again, I felt like I was reliving my mother's old life. I sat down on the sofa in the back of the dorm's lobby and began questioning if this was all worth it.

What am I really accomplishing by being in college if I still have to live in poverty? I wondered. After all, not only was I alone and poor, I was now kicked out of my own home by my stepfather. I had no one and I was penniless. At least if I drew welfare and food stamps, like my mom had done only a few years ago, I would have more than I have at this very moment.

But the thought of being on government aid forever was not even remotely appealing. I knew that in order to make it and break out of this vicious hold that poverty had on me, I had to pay my dues. Leaving college wasn't going to present an immediate fix to my problems. No — I had to hang in there for as long as I could because, like my mom had always drilled into my head, "You will only get somewhere in life if you have a college degree." I knew she was right. A college degree wasn't going to make me any smarter than the next person, but it sure gave me a chance at making my life better. Companies seemed to only reward those with a degree in the corporate world. They didn't have much to offer to those with just a high school diploma. Now was my only chance and now was as good a time as any. So, I summoned the courage to be alone and hungry for the next week, wondering how I was going to survive this next obstacle.

I tried not to linger in the dorm lobby too long on the last day of school before break. It was too painful and scary watching students leave, one by one. Often times, their families would drive in to pick them up. Watching them leave with packed bags left me feeling as empty as their abandoned dorm rooms.

By the end of the day, the dorm lobby had gotten quiet with the exception of a few lingering students who wouldn't be leaving until the next morning. The cafeteria was already closed to the student population, so my dinner for that night consisted of the food that I had taken during my last assignment working in the cafeteria. I had one piece of banana bread, some brownies, and a few leftover sandwiches that I had secretly made when no one was looking. It was all wrapped in paper towels and sitting on my desk, waiting to be rationed out. That's all I had, so I tried to stretch out my food and eat as little as possible.

The next morning was dead quiet in the dorm. I looked out of my window and all I could see was a light fog laying low across the grass. There were no voices in the hallway or cars driving by, like I had gotten used to hearing and seeing each morning. I looked out in the hallway and noticed that someone must have turned off some of the lights. Thank goodness they hadn't turned off all of the lights. I wondered if my RA had made sure of that when I asked her if it would be okay to stay in the dormitory during break. She had obtained special permission from the college since they were not used to having students stay behind. Then suddenly I thought I heard a noise down the hall from the bathroom. I quickly closed my door and locked it, realizing it probably was my imagination working overtime. To overcome the approaching fear and loneliness, I decided that I would put on a positive attitude and a coat and walk around the campus that I had come to love. It was so peaceful and beautiful with its protective trees. I figured I might as well enjoy what I could.

To my surprise and relief, I found that not everyone on campus had left. The library was open! If I ever felt scared or alone in my dorm, I could always go to the library and sit at a desk in the basement, losing myself in a *Life* or *Time* magazine. I also found that the mail room was still open, run by a couple of students who had stayed behind like me! I wanted to run to them and ask them what building they were staying at so I could visit and not be lonely anymore, but I didn't know these students. I only remembered seeing them in my classes. I also noticed that Dean Anderson was in his office, working as if it was just another school day. His secretary was there, too.

I remembered when he had helped me before with getting a new winter coat. I wondered if he could help me again. Since some of the buildings were still open during break, maybe the dean knew of some campus jobs a student could work to make some extra money. Maybe I could work in the mail room, too. If I could do that, I would solve my problem of affording food (that is, if they could advance me my wages). I shyly approached the dean's secretary once again and requested a visit. She quickly brought me into the dean's office and I was again face-to-face with the same kind face and brown hair. Only this time he wasn't wearing a suit—he was wearing jeans and a faded green sweatshirt.

I explained my situation to Dean Anderson, hoping he didn't think I was trying to take advantage of his kindness.

"I'm not sure about any jobs you could take in the mail room or in the library, but you could work for me. I have some things that need to get done as long as you don't mind if the tasks are a bit tedious," he offered.

I happily accepted his offer. Joy flooded my whole body. When I asked if I could request an advance on my wages, he immediately reached into his wallet and produced a twenty-dollar bill. A twenty-dollar bill! Now I wouldn't have to worry about food this week! Twenty dollars could go a long way for one person in a single week. I knew the foods to get to make the dollar stretch as far as it could. Instant macaroni and cheese that my mom always used to buy cost less than a dollar, and Kool-Aid packets were twenty-five cents as long as you didn't mind drinking it without the sugar. I had learned that from Mom, too.

I could barely summon the courage to look up into his face but I did anyway to thank him for all he had done for me. He immediately called his secretary into his office and explained the situation, asking her to put together a list of things I could do. With that, she and I left his office. Later that day I would return to start my job as "helper to Dean Anderson's secretary." I smiled, wondering how that would look on my résumé. I secretly said a prayer to God to thank Him for what He just did. I looked up into the sky hoping He could see my gratefulness.

Patricia Miller Mauro

To bide my time until later in the day when I would return ready for work, I continued my tour of the campus but this time veered off in the direction of the stadium and track. As I walked the track, I thought I could hear music coming from the fraternity house at the top of the hill. It was coming from a building called the Stag Club. It wasn't a national fraternity and was quite small, member-wise, compared to other fraternities. Their house was the grandest-looking of all the frat houses on campus. It reminded me of a large plantation house with its huge white pillars in front and black shutters at every window.

I directed my eyes toward the sound of the music and realized there was someone lying on a big red blanket on the roof. As I walked closer I could hear lyrics being sung by Karen Carpenter. I recognized the man on the roof as someone I had met in my accounting class.

Then I heard someone yell, "Patti! What are you still doing here?" It was Shamar, a student from India. He was the student who had explained supply-side economics to me in Cambridge Hall. I waved back and he yelled for me to come on in. So I did.

Immediately, I could smell the undeniable aroma of food cooking. I was shocked to find an almost-busy house full of students who were all from India. Before I could ask about their situation, a stout, middle-aged woman with dimples came out from the kitchen. She was introduced to me as Cookie.

"The boys were just about ready to sit down and eat. Would you like to join them? I cooked enough for everyone," she said as she smiled.

My First Break Alone

I liked her immediately and realized her relationship with "the boys" must have been close because one of them went over and gave her a big hug.

I gratefully accepted and sat down with Vivek, Shamar, Vijit, and the roof-dwelling student, Ranjit. Together, we were served hot roast beef, mashed potatoes with steaming gravy, fluffy biscuits, and chocolate cake for later. I stuffed myself with two helpings, saving my cake for the trip home. I figured I could add it to my stash back in the dorm room.

Over dinner, I asked them why they had remained back on campus. Each of their stories was similar: they couldn't afford the long trip back home to India, and so they almost always stayed on campus during breaks. The only time they did go home was during the summers. They asked me why I was still here, too, and I briefly explained that my family was away and that I didn't want to go home if no one was going to be there. I hoped God didn't mind my little white lie.

I was overjoyed because now I knew that I would no longer be the only person living on campus during a college break. If I ever got lonely, I could always come visit these students who I already casually knew from my classes.

Through my conversations with them, I also found out that Cookie, completely aware of their situation, always made a point of coming to the Stag Club before a holiday to cook enough food to last them for the entire week. She would show up and in one day cook enough food to last her boys until school started up again. For spring break, that was today.

As we talked over our delicious meal, one of the students said I could come visit them every day and eat with them, too, since I had no one else to eat with. Little did they know that my concern was not about having anyone to eat with—it was the concern of having no food at all to eat. I reached into my pocket again just to make sure I hadn't dreamt about that twenty-dollar bill. *Nope! Still there,* I thought to myself as I squeezed the crisp piece of paper. I couldn't believe how good this day was turning out to be.

After we all finished, I thanked Cookie and gave her a hug, too. For a quick second I had renewed confidence that I could actually survive this week. Plus, I still had the twenty-dollar bill in my pocket from Dean Anderson. My fears of being hungry and alone began to slowly diminish as I walked back to the main campus to begin my job.

Maybe I can actually do this, I thought to myself. My confidence began to soar. Even though I dreaded returning to a dark and empty dorm building later that day, I looked forward to the day when all of the students would return again. I imagined their voices in the hallway and the sound of cars driving by. Never again would I take the noises of school for granted. I just had to hold out for one week then my life could return to normal again. Until then, though, I had the necessary tools to survive and that is all that mattered for the moment.

Punctured Peace

It was the fall of 1985 when I sat one evening memorizing the various economic theories that I needed to know before Friday's midterm exam. I took a break from studying and began to think. I was good at thinking. Thinking was what I never stopped doing. I began to think about my journey to this point in my life and how my life was now.

Days and nights at college had transformed it into more predictable events. They were no longer peppered with unexpected outbursts or uttered resentments that seemed to endlessly issue forth from my mother's house. I had grown increasingly distant from my former family these past six months and so my evenings were a lot quieter and my conversations turned to being much more pleasant. I began to think of Muskingum College as my home and the students, faculty, and administrative personnel—even the cafeteria workers, students at the Stag House—even the protective trees that surrounded the campus. They all had become my extended family. It was almost amusing that they had no idea I had just adopted them, but I did. In my mind, this was my home for now and I began to feel safe in my environment.

I took a certain satisfaction in knowing that even though I had been kicked out of the house, I was surviving. I wasn't on welfare yet, I wasn't paying for milk with food stamps, and I hadn't been kicked out of college yet. I had even survived spring and summer breaks without the help from my parents and without going home. I even found a government-subsidized apartment during my first summer alone. All I had to pay for rent was twenty-six dollars a month plus utilities, and the place was mine for June, July, and August. Only a mile away from school, it was close enough to walk to my job on campus. I had been hired to help a geology professor sort through and categorize microscopic specimens he had gathered on various trips.

I was thriving in this place and was glad it was a whole hour away from where Mom and Bill lived. I had found some peace in the books I read, in the library basement, and in the offers from friends to gather to do anything fun like go bowling, eat out at a restaurant, or meet at someone's apartment to watch the latest episode of *Miami Vice*. I always had a steady campus job that provided me the monthly stipend I needed for things like postage stamps, makeup, or a little splurge here and there on a pair of earrings or on an alarm clock. I had decided to put my worries on hold about my campus wages. None of that was going toward my tuition bill like it was supposed to.

Punctured Peace

But I couldn't worry about that now. I had to worry more about those things that were affecting me now. I would cross that bridge when I came to it.

Every once in a while, however, my peaceful existence would be punctured by a call from my mother. She still made it a point to call me (without Bill knowing) to inform me of how desperate things were getting at home. I guess she also felt a need to continue some communication with me. After all, I was her daughter and she was my mother, and we had been through a lot together during some really rough times. I was always happy to hear her voice but, in a way, I didn't want to hear any more about Bill and how his temper really got the best of him last night when he punched in the closet door. I wanted to be done with the violence that seemed liked a way of life for him. But her stories continued and through them I began to believe that divorce was soon to follow. According to my mother, Bill had even left her for a few days to straighten out his thoughts and Kim had talked of moving out even though she was only sixteen years old.

Oh, how I missed and worried about my sister. *Why didn't I just bring her with me to college*? I thought to myself. But then, how would I have provided for her and for me? We couldn't have stayed in a dorm room, so we would have had to have gotten an apartment together and how would we have earned the money for that when I would have used the money for school books during the school year? As it always seemed to happen, I let my thoughts take over and they began to swirl in my head until I was practically dizzy.

Patricia Miller Mauro

I tried not to let my thoughts take me too far but I couldn't help it. I imagined Kim, sitting alone in her darkened bedroom, crying and shaking from the evils that lurked all over the rest of the house. I knew that the drinking had become worse. Mom's speech was sometimes slurred when we talked on the phone. When our conversation moved to Bill, every other remark out of my mother's mouth was pocked with curse words. If there was that much hatred spewed over the phone, I couldn't imagine the trials that my sister was going through. I wondered why I hadn't heard from her and that made me worry even more. Even though we promised to write each other, I hadn't received a single letter from her. All of my letters to her went unanswered. When I asked my mom about Kim, she would only mention that Kim had her own issues, as if she was contributing to my mother's problems. Clearly, there was no sympathy in her voice, and so that confirmed that my sister was definitely alone in all of this. What "this" was, though, I had no way of knowing.

During these times, it was hard to turn off the thoughts and refocus myself on my studies, but I had to if I were to get through college. I tried to look at the more positive side. I had many things to look forward to. In just another year I could finally declare myself independent, and all of my financial aid would be based on my needs and not on the income my parents made but didn't share. Once I reached that status, I could finally breathe a sigh of relief, because the path to graduation would be much clearer. Then I could graduate, get a job, and provide for my sister and mother. They could move out and divorce themselves from Bill forever, and our little family of three would be whole again.

In the shorter term, I could be glad knowing that every day, I could count on three square meals a day and that Sundays and breaks were tolerable if I followed the same steps I had laid out before. I had many more weekends to look forward to of bowling and eating with my friends. In a small way, I realized there were times when I could actually relax and act and feel like a normal college student. It was only during my mother's calls that I would be snapped back into the "responsible adult with no home in survival mode and not like any other college student" status.

With each successive call from my mother, I began to realize just how much closer she was to becoming a poor divorcée once again. Evidently Bill and Mom were discussing it with each other regularly. That thought chilled me to the bone. How would she manage with no money again? How would my sister take going back to our old life of poverty and shame? Even though I was mad at Mom for allowing Bill to make the decision to prevent me from coming home anymore, I still loved her and my sister, and I cared about them. My mother had sacrificed for years so my sister and I could have something to eat and a place to call home. I also never really bought into the idea that Bill's decision against me coming home was unanimous. It was more like they were going along with what was being decided for them. It would take a lot more than that to dissolve what the three of us had built together.

Patricia Miller Mauro

I had to keep doing what I was doing—I just had to. There was no way I was going to turn back now, not with the risk of slipping into a life of poverty again like I had experienced when my mom raised us during those years. There was no way that I was going to boil water for a hot bath again or hang blankets at every doorway during the winter to stave off the cold. I made up my mind that I would never look at another food stamp again. I wasn't going to beg friends and family for a twenty-dollar bill, and I wasn't going to sit in my tattered rocking chair and hyperventilate, like my mother had, in front of the policemen who were at the door, ready to arrest her because she had kited one too many checks at the A&P.

I was going to continue using what I learned from her on how to survive to up my own chances of survival. But that's all I would own from that past life. Outside of that, my mother's life of poverty would not be mine. If I could do that, I figured I could help her once I got out of college and got myself a good paying job. Then, maybe she could live with me, and I could take care of her and my sister. Then, finally, maybe we all could have the happy and peaceful life that always eluded us.

I imagined life after graduation, with the three of us sitting in our comfortably warm apartment, watching TV together and having a delicious dinner of lasagna or steak. We would have hot water for every shower and a brand-new washing machine and dryer, ready to wash our clothes. No longer would we have to soak our jeans in the bathtub with cold water and dishwashing liquid. More importantly, there would be peace in the house. No one would be throwing punches anymore and uttering endless threats about pulling a gun out from the coat closet. I imagined the three of us back together again and happy.

    I told my mom to hang on a little longer and spoke to her about my plan and my dreams of helping us all. I hoped my words would soothe her in a way that her glass of vodka could not. Little did I know that it was too much for me to ask that she wait another couple of years before I could make it. I was to learn soon that she didn't have that much time to wait. The future would come on its own impatient terms and I was about to learn a real life lesson on the meaning of the word *helpless*.

The Call Back

A whole school year had passed before I found myself in a town far from school called Rochester, New York, in the summer before my junior year of college. A friend from the Stag House and his sister (whom I had met in another social club at Muskingum) had decided to live and work in Rochester for the summer and asked me if I wanted to come along, so I did.

Where else was I to go anyway? I could do what I did the previous summer and live off campus and work at college or I could take my friends' offer and work in a new place that was far from Ohio. I looked forward to something different and agreed to go. Once we all set ourselves up in an apartment, I found a job as a waitress at the local Perkins restaurant. One downside was that my shift was from 11 p.m. to 6 a.m. every day. The other downside was that I had no car so I was forced to walk the two miles back to the apartment each morning. It wouldn't have been so bad, but my feet were not used to the constant standing and walking a waitress job demanded, and the blisters that formed on my feet seared with pain, especially during my trek home. But at least I was making money and doing it on my own.

While my friends worked their own day jobs, I usually caught up on my sleep on a twin mattress that lay in the living room corner. It was on one of these days that I awoke to the phone, ringing. I tried to ignore it, but just when it stopped it would start again and ring and ring until finally I lifted my heavy head from the pillow and in a sun-drenched haze, I answered. At first I didn't recognize the voice on the other end, but it was familiar — in distress as if on the verge of crying.

"Patti, you have got to come home. I really need you. Your mother really needs you."

I couldn't believe what I was hearing. It was my stepfather's voice. The last time we had talked was in a heated argument a few semesters before when I tried to borrow money from him. I remembered what he had said then: "You're just like everyone else, wanting money from me. The answer is 'No!'" I had slammed the phone down hard to that voice, and now it was back — pleading and almost desperate.

"What happened?" I asked, trying not to sound panicked, although my thoughts were running wildly this time. It must have been serious for me to get a call like this.

"Your mother . . . ," then he stopped.

"*What?*" I practically yelled. "What happened?"

"She has been drinking a lot lately. Well, she finally

had too much one night and she got in a fight with your sister. It was awful."

Oh, dear God, I thought to myself. I could only imagine what must have happened. *Where is my sister? What happened to both of them? Are they okay?* All I knew up until this point was that they were staying at Bill's cabin at Atwood Lake for the summer.

I asked Bill all of these questions. I found out that both were OK, physically. But the evening's events most probably left some heavy emotional scars in both corners. At least that's what I gathered in the five minutes we spoke. Evidently, Kim and Mom had a fight. Mom was drunk and mean. According to Bill, she punched Kim in the face and her wedding ring got in the way. As Kim ran out the door crying, Mom chased after her down the street, ordering her back. Kim had found refuge in one of the neighbor's houses but Mom had caught onto where she was. Barb and Dan tried denying to Mom that Kim was hiding in their house. Mom didn't buy it and circled their cabin, yelling her name, peppering it with expletives while Kim sat hunched in one of the rooms within clear earshot. The neighbors looked at Mom in disbelief and then they called the police. Mom soon found herself with the choice of either being arrested or seeking help. A short time later, she was admitted to an alcohol rehabilitation center called Glenbeigh. It was located on the outskirts of Columbus, Ohio.

Why no one had told me this before was beyond my comprehension because I found out that this all happened a month ago. Now, Mom was expected to be released from there in a week, and Kim and Bill were fearful of what they may encounter. Evidently, Bill needed me to come back and help him and my sister out with the house and to be there when Mom came home.

Tears began welling up in my eyes. How could my mother have lost so much control of herself and where was all of this anger coming from? Mom had never hit either of us, and now she was becoming a female version of Bill. Kim just happened to be in the middle of everything. Oh, how I wished I had been there to protect her. I wondered why I had left her to go to college. Maybe it wasn't all worth this. My sister was reliving yet another hell, and I wasn't there to get her through it.

"Kim and I really need you. Can you come home and help out?" Bill pleaded.

I immediately accepted, fearful of all that my sister had just gone through and what she might end up with once my mother was released. Would the fighting continue? Would it escalate into something even worse? Just when was this nightmare going to end?

That night I gave my notice to the manager at Perkins and worked my last shift. The next day I began the process of packing my things. I would leave Rochester and stay with Mom, Bill, and Kim until my junior year of college started in a few months. It felt strange, going back to a family that had disowned me. But, regardless, the duty to protect my sister prompted me to leave my friends and hop on a Greyhound bus the very next day.

After the tiring twelve-hour ride, I arrived at the Dover depot and was met by Bill. He picked me up and

The Call Back

drove me to their home in his Lincoln. The last time I had ridden in this car was in the backseat, holding a shaking violet on my lap. Now that seemed liked an eternity ago.

Bill was quiet on the ride home, but he did manage to inform me that he and Kim moved back to the house in Dover, at least temporarily until things calmed down. Once I walked through the front door, I was met with an eerie quiet. I quickly looked around the once-familiar living room. Now the room and this entire house had become strange to me. Bill left for a second, and I wandered through the house, looking for my sister, but she was nowhere to be found. In fact, the whole house was empty and I was a little relieved — better empty than filled with angry people, spitting words of rage at each other. I noticed dishes, stacked, along the kitchen counter, caked with the remains of food that clearly had been eaten days before. The dining room was dusty, as if the idea of a family meal was a long past memory. I peeked into Kim's bedroom and found nothing but a heap of clothes that was scattered on the bed and floor. The bed wasn't made, either. I wondered if Kim had made a hasty retreat that morning to escape her confines.

Bill had further informed me that Kim was working but would be home soon. He didn't tell me, though, the surprise I would find in her. All I thought of was sitting down with her and asking her if she was okay. I wanted to hold her again and let her feel a semblance of sanity and safety in my arms. But when she arrived home, none of that would happen. She walked right past me and into her room, shutting the door behind her. Shocked, I followed her and walked in without knocking.

"How are you?" I asked, not knowing what to expect. I felt like I was in a dream.

"Fine," she stated with absolutely no emotion. She didn't even look at me.

"What's going on?" I asked. I moved closer to her, trying to establish contact, but all she did was continue folding her clothes without even looking up.

All I could think of was that maybe Bill had turned her against me. After all, it had been clear to me that he and I definitely didn't get along. I wasn't allowed to come home anymore. Now, maybe his orders to her and to everyone had been, "Don't talk to Patti." I was surprised and angry that I was the one that was being ostracized over and over. What had I done to deserve all of this? Why would she go along with what he told her to do? We had such a strong bond that had been molded over all kinds of struggles and hardships. How could one person destroy all of that in only a couple of years?

"At least you could have responded to my letters," I said, ready to leave this unfamiliar room.

As I turned to go, I heard her say, "What letters?"

"You mean you didn't get any of my letters? I wrote you so many letters, and I never got one letter back."

"Pat," she said, "I never got your letters." I could see tears forming in her eyes.

I walked back over to her and grabbed her, pulling her toward me. She sobbed in my arms, and I was glad I had found my sister again. I held her for a long time while her shoulders shook hard.

We talked after that and I found out that my letters had been intercepted. I also found out just how bad it had gotten at home. It was then that I heard how Mom's drinking had gotten heavier and heavier, how Mom felt that Kim was siding with Bill on minor, everyday issues, and how the tension built up between them to the point where Mom decided to resolve everything with a punch to the cheek. This is exactly what I had been afraid of when I left for school. I just knew things would escalate. How was I to know that the next explosion wouldn't be even worse than the last one?

"I'm worried, Pat," Kim told me. "Mom is really bad off. I don't want her to come home."

Her lips curled up and she began to cry some more. I finally realized why Bill had wanted me to come home so badly. It appeared that both he and Kim were petrified of Mom, and they didn't know what to expect when she returned from rehab. He probably thought that with me home, Mom wouldn't go back to being her drunken, belligerent self.

I held my sister and rocked her, trying to instill some sort of comfort. I wondered why Bill had not reappeared, even when dinnertime had approached. Looking out the window at the setting sun, I noticed his car was gone from the driveway. Kim offered to drive me to the local diner for a hamburger. It was the place she told me she went daily for lunch and dinner. I suspected a total disconnect had been established between all members of the family. They just happened to live under the same roof.

Patricia Miller Mauro

For the next few days I focused on washing dishes, doing laundry, comforting Kim, and establishing some semblance of order in each room of the house. Just about everything had been taken care of by the time Mom returned on Wednesday. Kim and I anxiously stood in the living room as she was escorted in by Bill. When she entered the living room, I was struck by the change in her appearance. Her hair seemed dried out and was poking out from her head in all different directions. Her face was almost an ashen color and, for the first time, I noticed the wrinkles that were carved into her face. She looked old, withered as if she were a tree that was barely surviving without its roots. She brushed past us both, entered her bedroom, and shut the door. Kim and I looked at each other, wondering what these next few weeks would evolve into. I secretly wished she would stay in that room the whole time but, of course, I knew she would surface soon to eat, to go to the bathroom, or to do whatever else a recently-released rehabbed person does.

In a small way, though, I felt sorry for my mother. It seemed like her life had been an endless string of heartache, poverty, and struggle strung together by loneliness, shame, and helplessness. But why was she doing this to herself? Did life with Bill need numbing this much? I wondered if rehab had dried out all of her desire to drink. I hoped so. Maybe she was going to be like her old self again—the person who always rejected an offer of liquor, preferring a glass of milk over anything. At least, that's the way she was before she ever met Bill.

The Call Back

Luckily, whatever occurred between my mother and Kim did not resurface and was not revisited. In fact, neither Kim nor I talked to Mom that much. Most of the time, Bill and Mom talked to each other, and I was glad that they weren't fighting. It was odd to see them be civil to each other. In fact, they seemed quite happy being in each other's presence. It would have been a welcome sight, had it not been for the tension that seemed to simmer and bubble up between Bill and me.

"Clean the dishes," he had demanded one day as he and Mom once again started toward the door. They were leaving us to go to dinner at the lodge. There was no food in the refrigerator or the cupboards. Whatever had dwindled was not being replenished. But Bill and Mom didn't seem to care that we were left behind with nothing to eat that night or on any other night. The only recourse we had was relying on Kim's earnings from her part-time waitress job that paid for our lunch and dinners.

"The last time you cleaned them, I noticed you hadn't cleaned the paring knife right. While you're at it, clean out the refrigerator, too." I was startled by his demeanor. Just a few weeks before, he was begging me to come home and help. Now, his old self was returning.

With that, they both left. My anger lit into a blind rage and I wanted to throw something.

Is that why he wanted me to come home? To clean his house? The house I wasn't allowed in until he said it was okay? I thought.

Kim came over and comforted me this time. She must have sensed how I was feeling. I wondered if she also picked up on the fact that I felt hurt and betrayed that Mom let him speak to me that way. Would she ever put up for me? *Why did I ever come back to this place?* I thought again. Even though I was relieved to see my sister again, I secretly wished that I was back at my job in Rochester. I missed being able to earn a paycheck. I even missed my blistered, two-mile walks and the twin mattress in the corner of the living room. In reality, I missed my life that had grown independent from this place. It seemed when I was here, Bill had taken that away from me. Life felt dismal and pointless.

A week later, I suddenly awoke to a searing pain in the back of my mouth. My gums were swollen and I couldn't even begin to eat as the pain shot through my body like a lightning bolt. I couldn't imagine what had happened but knew I had to see a dentist right away. I asked Bill to loan me some money to make the trip to the dentist. I was desperate for the constant pain to subside.

He replied, "If you wanna make some money, why don't you try earning it? Go get a job. I bet you could babysit for the Wilsons up the street. They'd hire ya."

I was stung with his uncaring words.

"But you don't understand," I said. "I've got to see a dentist now — I'm in a lot of pain!"

"Then you better start looking for a job pretty soon," he retorted. With that he turned and left.

I hated him with everything in me. I wanted to transfer the pain I was having to him so he could once again come crying to me for help. I fantasized turning him away with words that would bite at him like they were biting me now. I briefly wondered what God would think of me now if He could see the seething rage and resentment in me.

Kim came over and put her arm around me.

"Come on, let's go out. I still have five dollars. That's enough to buy a couple of milkshakes."

I felt so bad that I was depleting what little money my sister had worked so hard for. My rage continued. Hadn't we already been through this before, wondering where our next meal would come from? For seven years, we worried on a daily basis about food. In college, I was forced to strategize about where my meals would come from on Sunday evenings and during breaks, all because I was refused any kind of assistance from my mom or Bill. Now here we were again, faced with the reality of our aching, empty stomachs. Bill and Mom couldn't have cared less—they enjoyed five-course meals at the lodge almost every night. What would Kim and I do for meals tomorrow?

With a wearied sigh, I followed Kim out the door. I hated the fact that I still had four weeks left in this place, and I wished I had never agreed to come here. I longed for the rolling hills and protective trees of Muskingum College again, and it seemed ironic that such a heavenly place existed only an hour away. How I wished I could escape and go there right now with my sister. But for now, I had to endure four more long weeks. I just had to take one day at a time, and before I knew it, my departure date would be here. I hoped for its quick arrival so I could say good-bye to this place forever.

Pain, Fear, and Loathing

At last! The check had come in the mail. It was the precious check that I had been waiting for during my days of agony. I vowed that once I received it in the mail, I would head right over to Dr. Walker's office to get my impacted wisdom tooth pulled. I didn't care how painful it would be. Anything would be better than dealing with the sheer agony daily. The minute I woke up in the morning, I was reminded of my worsening tooth, the awful pain, and my awful existence here in this house.

Like Bill had suggested, I had approached the neighbors and asked them to babysit their two daughters to earn the money I needed to go to the dentist. The neighbors eagerly agreed and, from that evening, I made a total of ten dollars. All I needed was thirty more dollars to at least put a down payment on a tooth extraction. That meant that I would have to round up three more babysitting jobs. But who knew how long that would take. Even if I had one job lined up each weekend, I still wouldn't have enough money for another month. There was no way I could wait that long. Each minute was a struggle in dealing with the pain. Mind over matter could only be taken so far until, by the end of each day, I wanted to grab my pillow, force my face deep into it, and scream as loud as I could. But I knew that wouldn't take the pain away. I realized I had to do something fast.

In my increasing desperation, I approached Bill one more time about my situation, and he still stuck to his suggestion for me to find a job. He seemed angry that I had brought the subject up again with him.

"What if I borrowed the money from my friend in Wooster?" I suggested to Bill. "Umesh once told me to write him if I ever needed anything."

"What the hell do you mean?" he angrily asked.

I couldn't understand why he would be so angry at such a suggestion. After all, it wasn't his money that I would be borrowing. It would be my friend's money.

"I don't care what you do to earn that money. But I don't wanna hear that you borrowed it from someone else, *do you hear me?*"

When he said that, his whole body shook, and he took a few steps toward me. I felt very threatened and backed off, telling him I wouldn't. I was afraid I would get punched in the face like the many times he had punched my mom.

Every time Bill yelled or commanded me to do something, he always had a knack for turning on his heel and leaving. Most of the time he left with my mom,

Pain, Fear, and Loathing

too, as if to say, "See, I have your family now and you're under my control!"

A few days later when I just couldn't take the pain anymore, I made the decision to call my friend Umesh in Wooster anyway, despite my conversation with Bill. He was a friend of one of the Stag Club members, and I had met him last summer when I stayed back and worked at college. We got along great and it was then that he offered to help me if I ever needed it. So, it was during this time that I decided to take him up on it. I was afraid of what Bill would do if he found out my decision, but the pain of my tooth was an even bigger threat. Not only could I not eat, now my speech was being affected because it was just too painful to talk. I nervously called Umesh when my stepdad was out of the house. I hoped Bill would not question the telephone number that I was dialing when he saw it in the next month's phone bill.

Umesh answered and my heart leapt for joy. It was comforting to hear a kind and familiar voice.

After the usual greetings I went straight to the reason for my call. He immediately agreed to send me forty dollars in the mail. I had hoped it would only take a few days to get here. I didn't know how much longer I could deal with this pain.

"Are you okay, Patti? What is going on?"

He must have detected the stress in my voice and noticed my attempt at hiding my slurred speech.

"Oh, nothing," I lied. "I just ran out of money and need something to get me through until school starts in a few weeks."

It must have worked, because he didn't ask me any more questions. We hung up after he assured me that he would mail the check that very day. I was so grateful once again for someone who decided to help me out in such need.

After I hung up the phone, I realized that I had totally gone against Bill's wishes that I not borrow from anyone. If he was threatening to me when he said it, I couldn't imagine what he would resort to if he ever found out I did this. To hide it, I decided I wouldn't tell him that I got the check nor would I tell him that I was going to the dentist. I would hide everything from him and let him forget it. If he asked me, I would tell him that the pain just went away on its own and that I wouldn't need to go to the dentist after all. I figured that on the day I got Umesh's check, I would go straight to the dentist's office and get my tooth pulled. Bill wouldn't know the difference if I stayed out of his way. I could stay in Kim's bedroom when he was at home then come out during the times he and Mom left together. He would never know and I would be free of this pain.

When the check finally arrived, I held it in my hands and stared at it. I couldn't believe I actually had the money I needed. I was so happy that I now had a way to ease my horrendous pain. I calculated that if I used Umesh's check for the dentist, I would still have the ten dollars left over from babysitting to help Kim pay for our nightly meals. Surely that would cover the cost of two dinners for at least a couple of days.

That afternoon I went to Dr. Walker's and, luckily, they took me right away without having to make an appointment. I just wanted to get the whole thing over with and as quickly as possible.

"How will you be paying?" the receptionist asked. Her brown hair was pulled up in a bun and her teeth revealed hints of yellow when she smiled.

"Well, I have this check . . ." then I stopped. For a brief second, I remembered back to the time when my mom had bought us groceries on credit and how I had ordered college books on the same principle.

"Can you bill me?" I slowly asked.

"Certainly," she responded. "Who should I address the bill to?"

"My dad, Bill Levenger," I said. I had purposely left out the word "step" in my response. I couldn't believe they were letting me bill the procedure, nor could I believe what I was doing. I was actually billing this to my stepdad. *Oh, what will he say? What will he do to me?* I shivered at the thought. I hoped fervently that the bill wouldn't reach him until after I had left for college—a time frame of two weeks. But I took the chance anyway. I shoved Umesh's check back into my purse and figured I would use it for school supplies instead—something I also desperately needed. My racing thoughts were suddenly snapped to reality when the dentist called me back into his office.

A few hours later, after my dentist visit, I lay on the living room couch while my whole face pounded with pain. The local anesthesia had worn off. I was happy that my tooth was finally gone but wondered if it was the right thing to do since the pain I was experiencing was even worse than it had ever been. *When will I be finally free of pain?* I wondered to myself. I figured I would lie down for a few hours before Bill got home. He was out shopping with Mom and it was late in the afternoon. Soon, they would come home, then leave right away again to go to the lodge for their regular five-course meal. I would sneak into Kim's room right before they came home and stay there until they left for dinner. For now, I took solace on the couch in the living room.

Just then, the door opened and there stood Bill with Mom standing behind him. His huge frame stood in the doorway and glared at me. I immediately jumped and sat upright, the pain electrifying my brain.

"What the hell happened to you?" he angrily asked.

For some reason, I felt he already knew. Anybody would have noticed just by looking at my swollen face. I couldn't lie. What if he found out I was lying? It was better to tell him the truth and face the consequences than lie to his face on top of everything else.

"I en to the denis," I replied. I could barely form the words with my swollen lips.

"You went to the dentist? *How did you get the money?*" he roared.

Shivers crept up my spine and tickled my scalp. *Oh God,* I thought, *please protect me.*

"I orrowed the oney," I tried to say.

"*Son of a bitch!* What did I tell you? How dare you! Who in the hell do you think you are? *I want you out of this house!*"

I immediately started to cry. How could he be so angry at me? Why couldn't he understand that I was in so much pain? All he could think about was how I went against his wishes. What stung even more was the fact that my mother stood behind him, not saying a word, even though his words were shocking, loud, and insulting. Why would she ever let someone talk to one of her daughters this way? She used to be so protective of me and Kim. Was this another change in her that I was supposed to accept as a result of her drinking? It was as if she had a lobotomy. Bill talked and acted for her and she just stood there.

"When you leave for Muskingum, I don't want you to ever come back here, do you understand me?"

I shook my head, crying hard.

With that, he turned and left with my mom again, slamming the screen door behind him. I fell face-first into the pillow I had been lying on. I screamed long and hard until I couldn't scream anymore.

There was no way I would ever come back to this hell on earth—never! I vowed that this would be the last time I would ever see these four walls again. I wished so hard that my friends from Rochester would be here tonight to come pick me up and take me back to my real home, to college. That is where I felt the safest and the most comfortable. It was nourishing for me to be there. Being here was where my thoughts turned dark like my parents, the type of darkness that would rot your insides out if you let it. I had to leave soon and looked forward to the day I would see my friends waiting for me in the

Patricia Miller Mauro

driveway. They had promised to come pick me up right before the semester started. I longed for that day.

A few weeks later, my wish came true and Umesh, Shamar, and Rashad were all waiting for me in their car. I had asked them to just honk their horn when they came by to pick me up. I had to tell them that because Bill told me under no circumstances were they allowed in the house. So, I had to meet them outside. I figured this was just another demand Bill was making to assert his control over me. I didn't care. I wanted to escape from this place as fast as I could.

I happily piled into the backseat. As we pulled away, I stared hard at the house that hid so much pain and misery from the surrounding neighbors. I worried for my sister, once again, because she was trapped in there with them with no hope of leaving for a while. I remembered back to my conversation with her the night before. "Remember, I'll be back for you," I had told her.

It wasn't until the door shut and we exited the city limits that my insides started to relax again. I was ready for another semester. I had taken Umesh's check and bought pencils, pens, notebooks, folders, and even a little blue and white pillow that I could put on my dorm bed for show. It wasn't until a few weeks later, during one of Mom's calls to me at school, that I found out that Bill had finally received the bill from Dr. Walker in the mail.

"Did you have that dentist charge Bill for your tooth?" Mom had asked.

I was a whole hour away in a school surrounded by protective trees and library shelves that would easily hide me if he ever decided to come find me. So, I replied yes.

"I thought so," she replied. She didn't sound angry or accusing. Just stated it as a matter of fact. "Bill was livid," she added.

I smiled because it was the one time I had finally gotten him back for all the things he had done to me. I had my school supplies *and* my tooth was gone.

And so was the pain. I was back in school and I was going to graduate. I would show him and my mom that nothing could stop me from moving forward. Mom could live with that miserable person for the rest of her life if she wanted. I would have no part of it. I decided that I would never again go back to that house and figured it would be a long time before I laid eyes on my mother again. At least, that's what I thought. What actually happened though would be something quite different.

A Leveraged Skill

College had become a refuge to me and was what I now called "home." I slowly shifted back into the familiar — attending classes, working in the cafeteria, and meeting up with my friends again. One thing that had changed now that I was a junior was that I was legally considered independent and that meant that all aid for school would be based on my own huge financial need. Grant money that I had never heard of before suddenly became available. I could now breathe a sigh of relief because my immediate concern was no longer that of being kicked out for not having a way to pay my tuition. Books for the semester were once again charged to my account in the hope that one day the balance would be magically taken care of. All I cared about for the moment was that I would have something to study from once classes began. My school supplies were already taken care of (thanks to Umesh's check) and I was more than ready to forge ahead. I was excited knowing I had made

Patricia Miller Mauro

the halfway mark to getting the bachelor's degree that I yearned to reference on my résumé one day.

If I could just last two more years, I would have my degree. I couldn't imagine it, though. It just seemed like such a far-off reality. But if I could do it, I would be the first person in my family to have a degree and I would finally be free from the risk of poverty, free from having to make choices I didn't want to make, free from my past. I could move ahead, give myself the OK to make my own future without anyone else's choices affecting it. Maybe one day I would have my own family and my children would not even know one ounce of the hurt, anguish, and poverty I had once endured. It was almost something I was afraid to dream of because the dream might not come true. But I had to try. So I continued on, happy to be a Muskingum College citizen once again.

One thing that I began to notice in my classes was that the professors would often require the students to use a computer to prepare their homework. The professor in my English composition class specifically stated that he wanted all papers in his class typed using the VAX 11/780 mainframe computers that had been set up in a separate room in the school's science center. I thought this was odd since all past assignments that we handed in did not have this requirement. Up to this point, everything had been handwritten. But for some reason, the professors seemed to have a special interest in the students getting to know how to use these computers.

As I began to use the computers, I noticed that I kind of preferred them over the typewriter and liked it much better than handwriting, too. Someone had coined the term "word processing" for what we all were doing.

Soon after the semester began, I found a new job on campus working as an assistant in Brown Chapel, the college's church. I looked for ways to use the skills I had learned with the computers. One time, when the chapel secretary was looking for a quick way to send out rejection letters to over forty professors who had all interviewed for an open position, I immediately thought of mail merging as a solution—something our English composition teacher had just taught us the week before. I checked out Mrs. Logan's typewriter and realized it had some programming built into it, including the mail merge functionality. I went to work getting those standardized letters generated with each professor's name and address printed at the top of each letter. Mrs. Logan thanked me profusely for saving her a lot of time. I made a mental note to somehow reference this new skill on my résumé.

The end of my junior year came as quickly as it started and before I knew it, I found myself with the dilemma of where I would be living and working during that summer. My friends from the Stag House, who I had begun to rely on heavily, had all graduated and switched from dreaming about getting their degrees to working in New York City and living their dreams. I dreaded the thought of being alone at school in my senior year because they had become my family, but a lot of them promised to stay in close contact with me, even agreeing to come back for my own graduation the following year.

Patricia Miller Mauro

I tried not to think about the fact that they were leaving and focused on the issue at hand.

At first, worries settled again on where I would live during the summer after my junior year. Luckily, I met up with another student who was looking for a roommate. In fact, she had become a good friend and was even in the same sorority I was in. So we agreed to move into an apartment together. I was so happy that I would know someone during the summer. Together, we searched and found an apartment just off campus. Now all I had to do was figure out how I would afford the monthly rent. I remembered back to the time when Mom was looking for a job. She, too, had needed a job and fast because she was running out of ways to come up with rent money. When combing the want ads in the local newspaper didn't work, she had resorted to a temporary employment agency. Surprisingly, they wanted to meet her right away. Once there, they interviewed her to determine the skills she had and placed her in a job the very next day. *Maybe I could do that, too,* I thought and contacted an agency located in Cambridge, the next town away.

After I interviewed with them and took word comprehension, filing, and typing skills tests, they said they would get back to me. Then I remembered that I almost forgot to mention my newfound computer skills.

"You know word processing?" the Manpower representative asked me.

"Yes," I replied. I looked at her and noticed a sudden flicker of hope in her eyes.

A Leveraged Skill

"We have been looking for someone who knows word processing," she said. "We could place you over at NCR starting next week. Would that be okay with you?"

My heart skipped a beat. I couldn't believe it! NCR! That was a major corporation with a well-known name. I could definitely put something like that on my résumé and whoever interviewed me would recognize that name immediately. The best part was that they were willing to pay me seven dollars and fifty cents an hour—much more than what I thought I could make. Last summer in Rochester I was only making minimum wage at Perkins restaurant and I certainly wasn't going to put that on my résumé. Things were looking up. I couldn't believe how quickly my newfound computer skills were paying off.

I quickly agreed to take the job and they assigned me as a word processor in NCR's quality control department. I reported to work in the car that one of my Stag House friends had given to me. Shamar had told me that he would have no use for a car in the big city. Everyone got around on the subway. It was an old Volkswagen Rabbit that had a hole in the floor on the driver side. When you drove through puddles you got splashed, but that was quickly rectified with a sturdy rug that served as a floor covering.

A few months later, with the summer almost over, I received a call from Shamar. It was exciting to get a call from the big city. He invited me to visit for a few weeks before the summer ended. Another friend, Viren, would be driving there by himself from Columbus. Shamar had talked to Viren, and Viren offered to pick me up on his way. I happily agreed, figuring it would be a nice change before starting my senior year in college. I gave my notice to Joanne, my roommate, and to my coworkers at NCR and prepared for my trip to the big city. I had no idea what to expect when I got there. A few days later, Viren came to pick me and together we drove into New York and to the apartment Shamar lived in, in a place called Astoria, Queens.

New York City wasn't what I expected at all, at least not in Astoria, Queens. The streets were very narrow and crowded houses lined them, block after block. The heat felt heavy the day we arrived. The smell of meat filled my nose as we passed Steinway Street. Viren told me I was smelling lamb from the many Greek restaurants we had just passed.

When we finally parked, it was in front of a drab brown brick building that looked to have five floors in total. As we walked up the stairs, I could smell more of that same meat smell and figured someone must have been cooking for dinner.

The apartment Shamar lived in was small and had two bedrooms. There was no carpet at all—only hardwood floors everywhere. I thought it strange that it didn't have carpet. Wouldn't the people below us hear our every footstep? I noticed that just outside the back of the building I could see an elevated train track from the bedroom window and, a few minutes later, a very noisy train stopped right in front of me. I heard a voice say, "Watch the closing doors," followed by a faint *ding-dong* sound. With that, the train rumbled off leaving rattled bathroom mirrors and knickknacks in its wake.

I also noticed that this apartment had no air conditioning as the sweat began to drench my clothes. I wondered if the heat was this bad on the lower floors. It sure was hot up here on the top floor. No wonder I could hear the train so clearly. Both bedroom windows were wide open to let in the stale air.

I tried not to let the living conditions bother me. Immediately, I began to strategize about getting a temp job here for the few weeks I'd be staying. There was no way that I was going to just sit around and do nothing. Although my friends suggested I relax and take in the sights, I was more interested in seeing how I could make a little extra spending money so I could get through my senior year at school with less stress.

So, remembering what I had done back in Cambridge, I looked up a temp agency in Manhattan. Only it wasn't Manpower. This time it was called WordForce. WordForce was a temp agency specifically devoted to people with word processing skills. At least that's what it said in the yellow pages.

Shamar made a point to take me there the next day. I felt bad that he had to waste his day taking me around but at the same time I was glad, too. There's no way I could have gotten around in this huge metropolis without a little guidance. Not only that, he told me he hadn't found a job yet either so he had plenty of time on his hands.

The next day, he took me to the train stop and we climbed the never ending stairs to the very top where the platform was. We waited for the same train that I saw from the bedroom window. It finally rumbled into the station, and I imagined it rattling the bathroom mirror and knickknacks back at the apartment. When we got on, I was hoping for a gush of air conditioning, but was met with the same stale air that seemed to envelope us everywhere. I looked around and noticed that every inch of the inside of the car we were in was either covered with an advertisement, some in English and some in Spanish, or different colored graffiti, which I could not read or understand. As the train started off, I was jolted by the sudden movement and grabbed the nearest pole. Sweat poured down the side of my body, and I glanced through the windows at the passing bedroom windows. We were off into what New Yorkers called "the city." We were headed to midtown Manhattan where WordForce was located.

When we emerged from the underground, I couldn't believe how different Manhattan was from Dover, Ohio. Buildings were so tall I couldn't see where their tops ended. People rushed by as if in a movie that someone had fast forwarded. I tried to stay out of their way as I ambled along, staring at everything and everyone.

"Patti, stop staring."

"Why?" I asked. Heck, there was so much to see.

"Because, you will attract attention," Shamar replied.

"I'm not allowed to look at people?" I said.

"Not unless you want them to look at you. If you want the attention, you will get it. Do not look at anyone in the eye, OK?"

A Leveraged Skill

I tried to understand but couldn't. I even said hi to a few people like we always do back at Muskingum but no one responded. I did get a few stares, though.

We finally found the building where WordForce was located and stepped inside.

Once there, I was treated to the same type of questioning, tests, and interviews as Manpower. Only this time the people I talked to had an accent that I wasn't quite used to.

"We got a job fo' you," the heavy-set lady in black spandex told me. "It's downtown at Chase. You can start tomorra."

"Chase? You mean the bank?" I asked.

"Yeah. That okay wichu?" she asked.

"Oh, yes, yes, that is fine!" I replied.

I couldn't believe it. I was getting a job at another big name company — twice within three months! Now I had another well-known company to talk about on my resumé.

"Um, how much does it pay?" I nervously asked.

"Nineteen."

"Nineteen dollars an hour?" I asked incredulously.

"Yeah, sweethot. You sure this is okay wichu?"

I nodded my head yes because the words just left. I couldn't believe that I could make that much money in one hour. But according to the lady, these jobs paid well because not many people knew word processing. I secretly wished my English composition professor was around, because I would have given him a big kiss. He had taught me a skill that evidently not many people

Patricia Miller Mauro

were onto just yet. But thankfully, I was one of the ones who did know and soon I would be reporting to a big skyscraper in downtown Manhattan for work. I thanked the lady in black spandex and walked out as if in a dream.

The next day, I began my official temp job as a word processor at Chase—one of the largest banks around. Even though it was a temporary job that was going to last for only a couple of weeks, I was thankful that I had this job at all. I could make some much needed money and take that back with me when I returned to Ohio.

They assigned me to a desk on the twenty-fourth floor. The office was comprised of about ten to fifteen desks all standing next to each other. When everyone was accounted for it looked like we all were working at a picnic table. The woman next to me was assigned the task of coordinating what I was supposed to do and I acted as her assistant. We worked on presentations for their training classes and I was asked to update their training classes on a calendar that detailed such locations as Jakarta and Hong Kong.

The job itself turned out to be very interesting, and I found myself training other employees in the art of word processing using their own Apple computers. I even taught them how to do mail merges and they seemed to really like the idea.

Finally, the vice president who occupied a corner of the floor in a spacious office with ceiling-to-floor windows, came out and requested that my work location be moved so as to accommodate a new permanent employee they had hired as a trainer.

A Leveraged Skill

"I don't have any more room for you right now," Sheila, the vice president said, "so hopefully you won't mind if I put you in this room."

She led me to an empty office down the hall that looked like hers except it wasn't a corner office. It had ceiling to floor windows with a big walnut desk and leather swivel chair. On the desk was an Apple Computer and behind the desk on a credenza was a big printer.

"You can work in here."

She smiled and left and I looked around, startled at my new surroundings. I turned my head slowly toward the door, half-expecting someone to pop their head in and say, "Hey! What are you doing in *my* office?" But that didn't happen and I slowly worked my way over to behind the desk and sunk into the soft, brown swivel chair.

I just couldn't believe my luck. Here I was sitting in an office in downtown Manhattan working as a word processor. I jumped out of my chair and looked out the window and noticed the spectacular view. Buildings of all shapes and sizes surrounded me. Just beyond them, I could see the glistening waters of the East River and boats traveling along it. Across the river, I could see Queens and was reminded of the train ride I took from there that morning. I was glad I wasn't stuck in that hot rumbling apartment watching soap operas. Instead, I sat here, daydreaming of what life could be like after college if only I could get my degree.

I imagined myself reporting to work in a place like this, complete with a suit and sneakers, just like all the women here seemed to wear. Once in my office, I would change into black glistening heels and report to my boss with the latest assignment or presentation. I imagined sitting in an office like this one, answering a ringing phone, and typing out documents on my Apple computer.

At lunch, I would don my sneakers again and head over to the pretzel guy on the street corner for some lunch. Working in the city began to take on a certain appeal. I remembered the comments my friends had made last semester about New York. They uttered words like "opportunity" and "career path." Maybe I could have a chance in a place like this. Not only that, I would be near my friends, too. Maybe I could live with some of them until I could get a solid job lined up. After all, New York was the city of opportunity. I got this job in a day without a degree—how long could it take to get a permanent job when you already had a degree? Suddenly, the dreams of my friends were fast becoming my dreams. I wanted to graduate and move to New York.

But first, I had to think of graduating. That would be the dream I had worked so hard for and I had to focus on that first before anything. But the dreams of what I might find here in the city gave me so much more hope.

It was just in time, too, for I was soon to learn that things at home were getting worse and worse as my mom slowly headed back to a life with no husband and no money. Soon, I would hear my conscience knocking at the door telling me about my duties as a daughter. Soon, my dream would change from getting a job to helping her financially so she would never have to go back to that way of life again. It would all happen—too soon.

Senior Year

I had a bad feeling about the last few months of my senior year of college. I should have been happy that I was only a short time away from my ultimate dream of graduating and getting my college degree. After all, I was all set, financially. All of my financial need for school was once again based on my own dire need, so the grant money was there for the taking. Not only that, I had some extra spending money as well from working at Chase Bank in New York City. They had liked me and I liked them so much that they took me back again, break after college break, to work a week or two here and there. After the end of each and every break I went back to school with enough money for airfare and a little left over for every day needs.

I was even able to line up an internship at Merrill Lynch, Pierce, Fenner & Smith in Zanesville for a few hours each week. It didn't matter that all they had me do was update their *Standard and Poor's* books with new pages they received in the mail. The important thing was that I could once again reference a well-known company on my résumé that could help me get a job after graduation. Now, the only hard part was getting through the year and it was already starting with some very bad news.

"Pat, I've got to talk to you," I heard my sister say on the other end. She had called me from her dormitory room at Kent State University. She was a freshman there. She, too, decided to heed the call my mother had made to us for many years and it echoed once again in my mind, "You must go to college! Do you want to end up like me?"

"It's Mom. Something terrible happened."

"What happened? Is she okay? Where is she now?" I asked frantically.

"She's over at the Tuscarawas County Mental Health Facility," she replied, her voice quivering.

Oh, no, I thought. *What could have happened to have caused her to be there?*

"She had a nervous breakdown, Pat," she continued. "She took an ax to the bathroom door, because she thought you and I were in danger. She called the fire department to report it. She thought you and I were somehow locked in the bathroom, and the house was on fire. When they showed up, they only found the damage she had done. When they found no fire and no one trapped, they took her away."

"How could this have happened?" I asked. I didn't understand that at all. I hadn't been at the house for a few months and Kim had left home long ago and finished high school while living at a girlfriend's house. I couldn't understand why Mom would think we were at home, let alone stuck in the bathroom with the house on fire.

None of it made any sense. She was alone when all this happened. I thought she must have been hallucinating. This was a new symptom to me. Usually, I had been associating her symptoms with drinking. Hallucinating had never been one of those symptoms. We were treading new territory and I suddenly felt nauseous.

I knew she had been going through a very rough time. Over the last few months, she and Bill decided to call it quits, and Bill had moved out. With everyone now out of the house, she was alone and drinking heavily all day and all night. I had visited her in late August to make sure she was okay, and I guess I should have seen the signs. Clothes had been strewn around, and dirty dishes were stacked on the kitchen counter. They looked like they hadn't been washed in weeks. *This is so unlike my mom*, I remembered myself thinking. She used to be so particularly neat and clean about everything. Now it was as if some other person had inhabited her mind and she was fast becoming a stranger to us both.

"When did all this happen?" I asked. My mind whirled with the news.

"It happened a few days ago. I just found out from Bill yesterday. Evidently the neighbors saw them take her away. I went there to look at the house myself. I saw the ax, Patti. I saw it, just laying there on the dining table. There was glass everywhere." Her voice trembled and I heard her take in a sharp breath of air.

I shivered. *Had Kim or I been there when she went over the edge . . .* , my thoughts trailed off. I had no idea if Mom was okay or where this place was where she was staying. All Kim knew was that they were transferring her to the Cambridge Mental Health Center next week.

"Cambridge?" I asked incredulously. "Oh, no." Cambridge was the next town away from Muskingum College. My psychology professor and college dean, the very one who had helped me so many times already, was affiliated with that place. What if he found out? What if the whole college found out and I was kicked out for having a mother who took an ax to her house? Immediately, I knew I had to find out where it was located so I could visit her the minute she got there. But, in a way, I was scared, too. Who had this person become? Would she respond to me? Was she coherent at all? Had we lost her forever?

I remembered a conversation I had with her back in August, my last visit with her. She was deeply depressed over her upcoming divorce. Thinking she probably was worried over her financial condition, too, I tried to console her by promising that I would help her once I graduated from college and got a job.

"Don't worry, Mom," I had implored. "I'll help you. I'll take care of you. I just need a little more time to graduate and get a job. Then we'll be home free."

"I'll be okay, honey. You girls just focus on getting through college. You both make me so proud," she replied with tears in her eyes.

I told her to hold on just a little longer and I would be back for her. It hadn't mattered that almost a few years had passed under Bill's order that prevented me from coming home anymore. I wasn't angry anymore at my mother for going along with it. After all, she did fight for Kim and me—Kim told me that later. Evidently, they continued to fight all of the time even after I left for college, which was no big surprise. But what did surprise me was that Mom had gathered the courage to fight for me, and my view of her began to change. I understood, in a weird and twisted way, that she didn't have much control in that relationship. When Bill drank, he was vicious and often resolved fights with a punch or a shove. On one occasion, the issue being discussed had culminated in Mom wearing a cast around her fractured wrist for six weeks.

She, my sister, and I had too much history together for me to ignore. I couldn't continue on with my life without any concern for her depressed existence. As her daughter, I felt my duty was to take care of her. After all, if it wasn't for her and her example, I wouldn't have gone to college and I wouldn't have known how to survive once I got there.

My thoughts snapped back to my conversation with my sister.

"Patti, are you there?"

"Yeah, I'm here," I said. I felt like I was in a daze.

"I have something else to tell you. Are you sitting down?"

What else could my sister tell me that could possibly top what she had just told me? Nothing could be so bad after the news she just delivered about Mom.

"I got in touch with Marvin," she said.

"What?" I replied, sure that I had not heard her right.

Marvin was our real father. For years, Mom had forced me and my sister to refer to him (if we had to talk about him at all) by his real name. Mom would never allow us to say "Dad" in her presence. That's how nasty their divorce had been, and the bad feelings stayed around for years. Mom had always threatened to disown us if she ever found out that we got in touch with him. I hadn't seen him since I was a little girl. Now, fifteen years later, my sister was saying that she had actually met him. I was astounded.

"Why in the world did you do that?" I asked. "You know what Mom would do if she ever found out?" I asked her.

Neither of us would have ever thought to go against Mom's wishes, that is, until now.

"I had to, Patti. You don't understand how bad things have been with Mom. I've seen more than you could ever imagine, especially during the last months I lived with her. Thank goodness I got out of there. I had to see him, Pat. I felt like I didn't have anyone else to go to."

I felt like I was in a dream and that I wanted to wake up from it all. Just thirty minutes ago, my life had been going along as it had for the past three years in a semi-functional existence. I wasn't sure I could take all of this news — this shocking, unbelievable news.

"He's nice. You'd like him. He wants to write to you. I gave him your number. Is that okay?"

Oh, dear God. What was I going to do? I didn't know what to say to someone I had dreamt about meeting for

Senior Year

years and years. I remembered my dad the most when I was five years old. He had been my absolute idol. He and I had done so much together. I remembered him teaching me how to hit a baseball in the yard of our Front Street apartment. I remember perusing the aisles at the grocery store during our weekly runs to Kroger. I remember running into his arms during one of the many camping trips that he had taken us on.

I remembered the night he said his final good-bye. He had his black- and red-checked hunting jacket on and he had tiptoed into my darkened bedroom late into the night to say good-bye. It was after he decided to give up all visitation rights. He couldn't take my mom calling the sheriff on him repeatedly every time he returned us to her a minute or two late. It hurt him that each and every time we went back to Mom she grilled us for hours on what Dad was doing and who he was dating. When we didn't have much to tell her, we were met with a spanking. When I asked her why we had to get a spanking, she would almost always reply, "Every time you return from your father's, you come back with an attitude." At the time, I didn't know what she was talking about. I would always try to answer her questions as best as an eight-year-old could. I told my dad about these grilling episodes with Mom, and the look on his face was one of sheer sadness. So, Dad decided to leave for good.

"Please don't go, Daddy," I had said to him.

"I have to sweetheart," he replied. "One day you will see me again."

I wanted to see him now, tomorrow, and the next day. I didn't want him to go away forever. He was leaving again and this time he wasn't coming back.

I wanted to see his face in the darkness but couldn't make out his features from the moonlight streaming in between the curtains. I remembered he hugged me for a long time and I cried.

I missed my dad so much during those fifteen years but as time went by, memories began to fade. I knew I loved him and that would never change no matter what bad things my mom had to say about him.

I remembered when he tried to send me and my sister gifts for Christmas. They arrived from the mailman, festively decorated in wrapping paper with red and green ribbons on them. But these were presents we were never allowed to open. Mom sent them back untouched, year after year. I remember staring at the wrapping paper thinking, *So this package was wrapped by my dad,* and I wanted to at least touch the gift to be close to him somehow. But that's as close as I ever got to my dad. No matter how many times I fervently wished to run into him at the library or the post office, I never did. Soon, my mom's comments about his regard for us began to take shape.

"He doesn't love you. If he did, he wouldn't have run off like he did. He would be here visiting you kids," she would always say.

Maybe she is right, I thought many times.

Now my sister was telling me that she had contacted the man my mother hated and who I hadn't seen for so many years. My feelings were a mix of anger, resentment, astonishment, and joy.

"He wants to meet you, Pat," she repeated. "I told him you were graduating in a few months and he and his wife Shirley want to meet you and come to your graduation."

My graduation? How would I swing that? What if Mom came to my graduation? She might be well by then. How could I possibly have both parents at my graduation? I couldn't even fathom the scene I knew it would create. I couldn't possibly think of having them both together. My mom would be livid if she knew we contacted him after all these years. But the thought intrigued me, too. What if I invited one and not the other? If I did that, who would come and who would not?

I hung up the phone with Kim and the room began to spin. I was sure I was hyperventilating and began to panic a little. My breath came in short, shallow spurts. How was I supposed to study and graduate with all this news? No amount of hiding in the library basement could protect me from what was coming. My thoughts followed me no matter where I went.

I steadied myself to get up. I'm glad I had sat down like my sister had asked me to. My legs shook and I felt like the floor would give way any second.

"Are you okay, Patti?" Terri asked. She was the neighbor across the hall in the sorority house we both lived in.

"I'm fine," I said with a forced smile. "Thanks."

I slowly walked up the stairs, opened the door to my room, and found the edge of my bed before I let myself sink down. I tried pulling myself together before that evening's class.

"You've just got to do this," I told myself. "You can't skip class today, you can't avoid Mom, and you better shape up because you've got to drive to Zanesville tomorrow for your internship."

I closed my eyes and hoped the spinning would stop, but even in the darkness of my mind I knew the furniture in the room was turning round and round like the thoughts that wouldn't end.

My Father

Only a few more weeks of this to go! I thought to myself. I was propped up on my bed, trying to memorize what goes into an audit checklist, but every time I read a few words, thoughts of my dad popped into my head, and the sentence I was reading ceased to have any meaning. I put my textbook down and wished I could trek across the campus to seek refuge in the library, but I was afraid of missing the call from my father—the one my sister forewarned me about. I had waited fifteen long years to see him and I certainly wasn't going to miss his call. I wondered, for the umpteenth time, what he looked like, what his voice sounded like, and what we would say to each other on the phone. My heart beat faster at the thought. It was a mix of anticipation and fear. *Mom must never know that I talked to Marvin,* I thought to myself.

"Paaaaaaattttiiiii!"

I recognized someone yelling my name in the haze of thoughts and memories that lay scattered across my mind in an unfinished puzzle. The voice belonged to Angie, another sorority sister. I hadn't noticed that the phone was ringing right before she called my name.

"Whhhhhaaaaat?" I yelled back, peeking my head just outside my door.

"Someone on the phone for yooooouuuuuu!" was the reply.

My heart immediately began beating so fast I thought I would be dizzy again. *This must be him*, I thought. I wasn't expecting any calls from my mom, and my sister and I had just spoken yesterday. Yes, this had to be my dad. I took a deep breath and swallowed what felt like a rhinoceros.

"Hello?" I meekly said into the phone. I pressed the phone hard into my ear. I wanted to hear every word, every breath from the man I yearned to see for so long.

"Patti? This is your dad, honey."

Tears began to well up in my eyes. He had called me "honey." I couldn't remember when the last time a parent had been that nice to me.

I had guessed that he detected my wavering voice as he calmly and gently told me how he had met Kim. He went on to describe how she had driven up to his driveway, got out of her car, and introduced herself to Dad just as he was installing a new garage door. They both hugged each other, laughing and crying at the same time. He told me that he had hoped and prayed we would find him one day.

Do you know how much I cried for you? I secretly thought as the gentle voice on the other end continued.

My Father

Where have you been all these years? Please, please don't go away again, Dad. I love you. My thoughts seemed to want to burst forth like a spectacular fireworks show. They pleaded to be heard in words but I put them away for now, hopeful I could give them a voice once my dad and I became acquainted again.

How odd it felt, sitting in the corner of my sorority house, gripping the receiver so hard that my knuckles looked white as my sorority sisters laughed and played music in the background. During our conversation, Dad and I had agreed to meet the following weekend for lunch. My first reaction was sheer joy at the thought of meeting my father after so many years, but when I hung up the phone my stomach churned. I wanted to see him, but I didn't know him anymore. He was now a stranger to me. Would we get along? Could we love each other the way we had when he had taught me how to play baseball in our yard on Front Street?

I stood on the porch of my sorority house dressed in white pants and a lavender sweater and waited for my dad who I hadn't seen in an eternity. I wondered what we would talk about, what he looked like. I was a little nervous, too. What if lunch with them would be quiet and awkward? Marvin and his wife Shirley were going to take me to a place called the Buxton Inn in Granville, Ohio—not too far away from college. I made a mental note not to call him Marvin like I had been coached to do for so many years now. Would it be too presumptuous to call him Dad? Oh, what my mom's reaction would be if she knew what I was about to do. I remembered back from years ago when she had threatened to disown me had I even considered getting in touch with Marvin again.

My thoughts traveled forward to the present. I continued to wait on the porch of the sorority house in anticipation of my father's arrival. I reflected on the conversation we had when my dad called after so many years. His voice was soft and gentle and caring. It didn't match the voice I thought he would have based on years of comments made by my mother. I expected a different voice — one belonging to someone who didn't care about his daughters or someone who left us willingly.

I looked forward to lunch with anxious anticipation. It would be the three of us together, and I would be with him them all afternoon. *This is far better than a chance run-in at the library or post office,* I thought to myself. The idea of whether to invite them or my mom to my graduation came up in my mind over and over, and I knew I had to make a decision about that since that was only two months away now.

I was surprised that I had recovered so quickly from my conversation with Kim, the phone call with my dad, and my visit with Mom in Cambridge these past few weeks. There had been a few times that dizziness suddenly set in on my walk down the hall on the way to accounting class or during the professor's lecture in statistics. When that happened, I tried to pull myself together and quickly realized my nerves were getting the better of me. I had to keep it together. I almost flunked my accounting class because I was forced to postpone the midterm due to the onslaught of dizziness and hyperventilation that seemed to kick in unexpectedly and more often than ever now. Somehow I managed to persuade the professor to reschedule my exam and I was able to take it and pass, but just barely.

I couldn't keep my mind on my studies and each weekend was spent visiting Mom in the mental health center in the next town over. She was coherent, but paranoid and depressed. Her appearance had changed quite a bit, too, and most of the times her hair was disheveled and her clothes dark and wrinkly. I guessed I would have been depressed, too, if I was locked up in there. It was an unwelcoming place with little brick houses dotting the grounds. The entire compound was surrounded by wire fencing. Other people there who she counted as friends walked around as if in a daze and I wondered how they even related to each other to form any kind of friendship.

With each and every visit with my mother, my anxiety seemed to gain new momentum, which I further fueled by my worries as to whether I could graduate or not. I was beginning to doubt my ability to hang in there for just a little longer and not let my nerves get the best of me. But the dizziness and anxiety continued. Almost daily, I was having what seemed like little panic attacks where the walls would suddenly start to float and the floor would shift as if attached to nothing. I willed my surroundings to not take any more liberties. I couldn't bear a scene where I would most certainly fall to the ground if walls and floors began to actually spin. I knew if that ever happened, I would lose control and where that would take me, I didn't even want to think about.

    I had to concentrate and not flunk any of the exams that would sink my whole future. Graduation was like a big ship blowing its horn because it was about to leave port. I imagined my graduating class on that boat and I could see myself running toward it as it is leaving for the land of opportunity. But with each sob from my mother, each visit I had with her, each dizzy attack and rescheduled exam, the boat seemed to float further and further away. I didn't even want to think what might happen if I missed that boat. It was going to my future and I just had to be on it, because what was left for me here? I would have nothing but a life of loneliness and financial hardship. It would be a repeat of what my mother had once lived and would soon face all over again. I didn't want to live her lessons anymore. I wanted to change them once and for all. I wanted to change everything and start over, creating as much distance from the past as I could.

    I covered my head with my hands, hoping I could deflect all the thoughts that never seemed to leave me. I half-amusingly imagined myself wearing a thought-deflecting helmet. *If only I could have one of those,* I thought some more. Then worry would hit the helmet and bounce off, landing on that rock over there. Anxiety would ping across the yard. Thoughts of Mom would drip from the helmet every two seconds like unending rain and graduation would finally land on top of my helmet like a large beam, cracking my helmet wide open.

My Father

Suddenly, in my peripheral vision, I saw a burgundy car slowly moving up the street toward the porch I was standing on. I looked over and just knew it was my dad and his wife. My heart seemed to leap with fear and happiness at the same time and the butterflies in my stomach bounced off every internal organ I had. They slowed to a stop. My breath started coming in short bursts again and I made a quick prayer to God to not let dizziness or panic get in the way of this day—this very important day.

After a few moments, my dad stepped out of the car and walked towards me. He looked so different from what I remembered. His hair was a salt and pepper color, and he was sporting a moustache that harbored a wide smile. In a matter of seconds, I became his little girl again and walked into his embrace as he uttered, "Hi sweetheart." All of my misgivings and resentment melted with those words and tears began to well up in my eyes. Shirley was right behind Dad. When we finished hugging, she stepped right up and hugged me, too. I liked her immediately.

Together, the three of us got into the car and drove off toward Granville for what turned out to be a memorable afternoon of lunch and catching up on years and years of lost memories.

It was also a chance to clarify some things. From our conversation, I found out that not a lot of what Mom had told me throughout the years was true and it was nice hearing the other side of the story for once. The most important thing I found out was that Dad was about as tortured as I was from being unable to see each other for so many years. Dad had visitation rights with us years ago, but with each visitation came a new series of fights between my mom and him. He told me that Kim and I had been dragged into the middle. To avoid any more hurt to us, he gave up his visitation rights, hoping that one day we would reunite again. I knew there had been an explanation. There just had to be. I looked over at Shirley for confirmation of what Dad was saying and she looked at me and nodded her head yes with tears in her eyes. I tried not to cry. It had been so hard all those years to dismiss Mom's claims that he wanted nothing to do with me or Kim. I wanted nothing more than to believe that it wasn't true. Now, the truth was coming out and it was what I had hoped for so long.

Then Dad leaned over with his wide smile, and whispered, "I have something for you, honey."

He reached into Shirley's purse and pulled out what looked like a Christmas present. I recognized it as one of the presents I wanted to touch but my mom hadn't let me. It was covered in faded Christmas paper and the green ribbon on it was crinkled. My hands shook and I reached over and cupped it, as if holding a little bird.

"Go ahead, sweetheart, open it," he added. A tear slid down my cheek as I carefully pulled away the present's covering that had been there for so many years. It was a small, orange transistor radio, the kind that looked like it was from the sixties or seventies.

"I wanted to give this to you when you were smaller. I figured a radio...," then his voice cracked and he stopped.

My Father

"I know, Dad, I know." I looked at it for a long time. I made sure to remember to keep the wrapping paper and ribbon, too. I didn't want one shred of paper or bit of ribbon to be misplaced any longer. I wanted it with me forever.

Both Dad and I cried, laughed, and reconstructed all that water that was under the bridge that day. It was our way of patching together a history we didn't have so we could move on and build off of that.

Much later that day, Dad and Shirley returned me to Muskingum College, where they presented me with an early graduation present. It was a burgundy Stebco briefcase. "For your new job," Dad said with evident pride. I imagined myself carrying it as a new member of the workforce, wearing my suit and tennis shoes on the way to work. I wondered what type of job I would be going to, but that was yet another bridge to cross later on.

After another hour, we parted ways with the promise that we would see each other again—on my graduation day. I had made the decision within the first hour of our meeting. I had no idea how I was going to break the news to Mom. I didn't have to worry about her suddenly showing up at graduation because she was still in Cambridge. For her to attend, I would have to obtain permission from the center to have her released for a few hours then pick her up in her own car. It was the car she had lent to me for my internship. She had been kind enough to let me use it since the car Shamar had given me the year before had long since broken down. Now, I had to call her and tell her I would not be picking her up after all. How I was going to do that, I didn't know. Even though my mother had her own hardships at the moment, she was keenly aware that I was very close to realizing the dream she had for me for so many years. She would often tell me how proud she was of me and how she couldn't wait to see me graduate.

But I wanted my father to be the one at my graduation. We had missed so many things together already. I wanted to pick up where we left off immediately. I wanted him to see me walk up and receive my degree as any proud father would. I didn't want to miss one more minute of living in the past where we were not part of each other's existence. *It will be the first thing I will change,* I thought, in this new life I was forging.

Oh, how am I going to phrase this to Mom? I thought to myself.

Guilt immediately set in, and I realized I was choosing someone else over my own mother. If it weren't for her, I wouldn't even be in college. She is the reason why I went against all odds and she is the reason why I survived it. Now, I would be betraying her. I just couldn't tell her that I had invited Dad, let alone tell her I had gotten in touch with him again after all these years. It would be a hurt for her that might be too much to bear. I couldn't tell her, not when she was already in a weakened state. Who knows what she would do if she heard what I had done.

I sat on the corner of my bed and tried to imagine how I would phrase this to her and what excuse I would come up with for not including her at my graduation. My thoughts whirled once again. *How can I possibly do this without hurting her? Will I survive these panic attacks and graduate? Will I make that boat after all?*

    I reached over for my briefcase and smelled its newness. I opened it up and imagined my work papers stacked within it. I fantasized about walking to work on a sidewalk in downtown New York, carrying my Stebco briefcase. I wanted to make my parents proud of me. I wanted to change the future forever. I yearned to be financially secure at last and wanted to provide that same security for my mother once her divorce from Bill was final. I just had to pass my exams one last time and then I could graduate. I closed my eyes and prayed hard for a miracle.

Graduation

It was Saturday, May 14, 1988, and I was sitting in the stands of the Muskingum College Recreation Center with my fellow graduates. In my hand, I held a piece of paper. On it, it read, "Muskingum College, upon recommendation of the faculty and the Board of Trustees confers upon Patricia Ann Miller the degree of Bachelor of Arts . . ."

I had officially graduated from college. I was a college graduate! I couldn't believe it. I had weathered the anxieties that seemed so overwhelming and I had graduated. It all felt so dreamlike on this warm, sunny afternoon. I looked over at the audience and tried in vain to locate my dad, his wife, and a few friends from the Stag Club who had flown in from New York for the special event.

I wondered if the graduates surrounding me felt the same way I did. Pride, disbelief, amazement, and joy filled me with anticipation for the next phase of my life: New York City. I had already made arrangements with a few Stag friends to live with them in New York right after graduation. They readily agreed when I approached them and I knew my next big hurdle would be getting a job there. But for now, I was happy in knowing I had accomplished one of the biggest dreams of my life.

I was already imagining myself getting a job the moment I got to New York. After all, it took only one day for me to get a job at Chase on my first assignment with them, even though it was through a temporary agency. Maybe Chase Bank would hire me since I had worked with them for so many breaks already. But Chase didn't seem to hold out much hope for me. When I had mentioned to them I was graduating, all they did was offer their congratulations. When I asked them about potential job openings they didn't offer to help me in finding one or in offering any type of job in the department I had helped out.

Well, at least I will have that experience on my résumé, I thought.

Maybe another company called DTC (Depository Trust Company) would offer me a job. Just a few weeks before, I had shamelessly called the company's CEO. He had served as speaker at one of the college's spring economics banquets. He was a "Muskie" alumnus, I found out later. What better way to shore up some business contacts than to call a fellow Muskie? He had told me during our phone conversation that he would meet me once I got into New York to discuss job opportunities. I

Graduation

hoped he hadn't heard my noisy sorority sisters in the background.

Meeting the CEO at DTC will be one of the first things I do when I get there, I thought to myself. I didn't want him to forget about me or our conversation.

After the graduation ceremony, everyone in the audience clapped for a long time and I tried not to shed tears. I wished my mother could have been there to see me but maybe she was better off where she was for the time being.

I tried not to let a tear slip down my cheek as I remembered our conversation the other night. She had been devastated when I told her I couldn't pick her up for the ceremony. I had lied to her and told her the car she had loaned me stopped working. I didn't offer to have a friend drive to go get her, and I didn't offer any other suggestions either. Her response to my story was a weak, "OK." That's it. Then I heard her start sniffling and I knew I had made her cry. I hung up quickly because I couldn't take it anymore. I, too, had to cry. The minute I hung up I ran to the room, closed the door, and melted into hot tears. I cried hard for the lie and the hurt I just gave her. I cried hard for all the times she had pushed me to get this far. I cried hard for all the skills she had taught me that I used to survive. And so this was my thanks back to her—a lie and a huge disappointment that she would never see her daughter graduate.

I tried to get my mind on something else and searched the ceremony crowds once more. I tried remembering all the times I was so sure I would be asked to leave this place. Somehow, I made it through, and I made a silent prayer to thank God for everything. I felt like one of those little birds He takes care of. I could do nothing, not even fly, without Him.

Later that night, I began to pack my things back at the room. Dad and Shirley had left with the promise that we would again meet up once I got settled into my new place in New York. My friends who already lived there had come to see me graduate and would take me back with them to live where they lived now. I would be living in the same apartment I had stayed at during my college breaks when I worked at Chase. My new address would change from New Concord, Ohio, to Astoria, Queens, New York, in a matter of days. I felt remorse for leaving Muskingum College. It had been home to me for a full four years. It was the longest I had lived anywhere in my entire life. It was the place that hid me from all my troubles and protected me so I could focus on changing my life. I would miss Professor Thomson and the quirky trivia he brought up before each economics class. I would miss Cambridge Hall where the other students and I congregated and studied each night. I would even miss the crooked streets that meandered throughout the campus. So much of the environment was quaint and quiet and peaceful. I doubted I would find many of those qualities in Queens.

That night, I made one last trip to the basement of the library. Finding an empty desk was no problem at all since almost all of the students had already left campus. I chose a solitary desk between two high stacks of shelves filled with periodicals. The room buzzed from the fluorescent lights above. I sat down and looked around, but didn't see any usual student activity. As usual, my eyes were focused on what my mind was replaying in my head, and I began to recount how very scared I was when I first became a student in this college. How things had changed.

I no longer feared my stepfather. My anxieties about affording college had melted away, and my panic of possibly not graduating was no longer a reality. I had finally made it. I had my degree and it was the key that would change my life once and for all. It was decided. I would not live my mother's life. I would not have my phone turned off. I would never hover over an electric heater for warmth in the winter ever again. I would never have to worry about where the rent money would come from. I would never again feel the shame of paying with food stamps. From now on, I would be able to live like a normal person.

As I got up, I looked around one last time and felt a twinge of insecurity. I was leaving the protective arms of Muskingum College. There would be no Dean Anderson in the real world. There would be no work study program in Queens. I couldn't take food anymore from the cafeteria on Sundays and I couldn't claim independence to gain the financial assistance I needed to keep on living. I had to find a job as soon as I got to New York, I just had to. My share of the rent and utilities would be due shortly and my college loans had to be paid. And there was a lot to pay.

Patricia Miller Mauro

I walked slowly back to my room to finish packing. The night air was quiet and the stars were out. I breathed Ohio in deeply, not knowing when or if I'd ever return and tried to rejuvenate my mind for this next phase of my life.

The Big Move

On Monday, May 16, my Stag friend, Shamar, helped me and my sister load up my mom's car in the driveway of my sorority house. Now that it was summer, my sister was left with the same question I had asked so many summers before: where should she stay? My answer to her was to come with me to New York and live with me, Shamar, and his sister Kavita in Queens. After the summer, Kim would return to college and I would stay on to begin my new life in the big city. Kavita and Shamar lived in the same apartment I had stayed at when I worked at Chase Bank during college breaks.

It turned out to be a much rougher summer than I would have ever imagined. Originally, I thought I would be able to find a job fairly quickly now that I had a college degree. For some reason, I thought I would be in the clear as soon as I graduated. That assumption was soon proven wrong and I found myself once again getting a temporary job through yet another temp agency. I didn't have the luxury to look for weeks and weeks for that perfect job. My first goal was to make money.

Many times I was reminded by Shamar's no-nonsense sister that our share of the rent was due. She also reminded me and Kim that if we were to eat, we would need to buy the food. She kept no food in the refrigerator since she spent almost the entire day working in a midtown hotel. The only time she came back to the apartment was to sleep.

Kim and I were used to bending to other people's wishes. Not only that, Shamar and Kavita were nice enough to let us stay with them so the least we could do was to try to find a job and pay for what was our share of the rent and utilities.

The temp job assigned to me was at Bankers Trust Company on Park Avenue. Once again, I relied on my word processing skills to persuade the temp agency to select me for the job. I say "persuade," because more and more people were gaining those precious computer skills that I already had. Computers were becoming quite commonplace and so my skill wasn't quite as valuable as it used to be. It showed in my weekly paychecks.

My sister Kim found a job with the same hotel Kavita worked at. So, by the second week of being in New York, both of us were earning money and contributing toward the household. We were safe for the moment.

But my job at Bankers Trust was turning out to be a nightmare. My duties were to act as receptionist for four investment bankers. Three of them were a pleasure to work for. I was informed by the people on the rest of the floor that the fourth man had managed to successfully run off half a dozen girls before me. So, to start off, I had a fear of this man and no one to train me.

Day after day, I began noticing a pattern with the fourth man, who was named Tom. The day would begin pleasantly enough with a "good morning" as he rushed into his office. But the instant he had an assignment for me, he turned it into an opportunity to berate and humiliate me in front of the whole floor. Words like "unreliable" and "incompetent" recklessly flowed out loud toward me, both in his office and more so out on the floor so everyone else could hear. Some days, I just barely made it to the restroom before the tears flowed. I didn't want him to see that he was getting the better of me. The other managers I worked for often commended me on my hard work and seemed happy with what I provided them. But this manager owed up to everyone's warning and found that nothing I did would make him think I was even worthy of working there. Day after day I began wondering if I belonged in the workforce. The confidence I had grown over the last four years was slowly being eroded. Familiar thoughts of "You're just not good enough," began to creep back. My past ghosts were looking for me again.

After work each night I would dejectedly head home on the subway and wonder what I had gotten myself into. New York didn't seem to be the solution after all. Many times I cried on my sister's shoulder and I felt embarrassed. I was supposed to be the big sister. I was supposed to protect her. But my resolve and will were wearing down fast in this hot, meat-smelling apartment that shook with each and every train that stopped and started right outside the bedroom window. I wished for air conditioning, a bigger paycheck, and my safe and quiet environment back at college. I felt I missed my chance at getting the dream job I thought would be waiting for me right after graduation. Where had it gone?

I had already met with Bill Dentzer, the CEO of DTC, during my first week in New York. He had told me about a possible employment opportunity in his company for a management trainee. But he said he wasn't sure if funding for the management trainee program would be approved this year. He would need the funding for this program if he were to offer me a job. He referred me to the human resources department to let them continue their communication with me about the program. If the funding came through, I would have a job. It would be salaried, and that was the type of job I needed. It also provided an opportunity to move up within the company ranks once two years' worth of departmental rotations were completed. Usually, after a particularly bad day at Bankers Trust, I would call DTC's HR department to see if the funding came though. All they could say was, "We're still waiting. We'll let you know," which to me meant, "Don't call us — we'll call you."

But with each successive week at Bankers Trust, I grew more determined than ever to hound DTC until they made a decision about my situation.

At the same time, Kim was having terrible nightmares night after night. Oftentimes she would dream about our

The Big Move

life back where we lived in Dover with Bill and Mom. When that happened, I would tiptoe over to her and put my arms around her and rock her, telling her it would be okay. And so it went: Kim was my solace during the day, and I was hers during the night.

Oh, when will our situation ever get better? I asked myself as I sat sweating on the hardwood floor next to Kim one night. It was where her mattress lay. I wondered how long I could hold out. I was afraid DTC would tell me they had no need for me. I was afraid I would be fired at Bankers Trust for being unreliable and incompetent although, for the life of me, I could never quite figure out why those had been his sentiments. Why would such a person berate me like that when each and every assignment was done on time and correctly? Is this what a person was to expect after working so hard for four years in college? Is this the life my mother had meant for me to have? This wasn't that much better than what we had back in Ohio.

Then one day I called DTC, expecting the usual answer of, "We'll let you know." However, I got a different reply of, "Yes, Patricia, funding has been approved. Your offer letter has been sent to you via FedEx."

I couldn't believe it! I was hired? I was going to be a professional! I was going to walk the streets of New York in a suit and sneakers with my burgundy Stebco briefcase filled with working papers. I found out the news right before my lunch break. I had called DTC from Bankers Trust in a hushed voice. I didn't want Tom to hear what I was saying.

I sat there, stunned. Was my dream on its way to becoming a reality? Tears of happiness filled the recesses of my eyes. I just couldn't believe it. This morning my life had been dreary and almost hopeless and in one phone call, my dream had come true, my life had changed.

But now I wanted to barge into Tom's office and, with a mightier voice than he had, announce my departure. The problem was that he was in another meeting on a different floor. It would have to wait. But I couldn't just sit at my desk that would soon again be empty. I felt I would explode with the unbelievably good news.

So, instead of sitting there, I excused myself and went on a two-hour lunch break. Across the street was a restaurant called The Bull and Bear. I went in and was seated at a large rounded booth with a white tablecloth on it. Normally, I would never have frequented such a place. This was a restaurant for broker dealers, investment bankers, and the like. But today I was going to treat myself because I finally received the good news—a reward for a degree hard fought for—and a job! I proceeded to order filet mignon, mashed potatoes, asparagus, and a glass of white wine. This would be my celebration lunch. I hoped while I was treating myself Tom would come back and find that I had completely overextended my lunch hour by a whole sixty minutes. What would he say? You're fired? I laughed at the suggestion.

But when I did go back to the office, he didn't seem to notice at all because someone was in his office for yet another meeting. Soon the person left and I waltzed into his office.

The Big Move

"I just wanted to let you know that my last day will be this Friday. I got a real job," I stated. I quickly became embarrassed at my last words.

"Oh, I guess you're better off not having to watch a group of boy scouts like us," was all he said.

"Yup," I replied. Then I left. I was surprised at his reaction since I was only there for two months, but maybe he was used to people telling them they were leaving.

After work, I went straight home to share the good news with Kim. We both laughed and hugged each other tight.

"Oh, Patti, I'm so proud of you," she said.

That night, I couldn't sleep from the sheer excitement of things to come. The walls were shaking; my body was sweating; and the train outside was once again instructing, "Watch the closing doors," but I didn't care. I walked over to the kitchen to get a drink of water. When I turned on the lights, all the roaches scattered to unknown places.

I couldn't wait to start my job, save my money, and move away from this place to a nicer part of town. I couldn't wait to save enough money to start sending some of it home to Mom. She was on her own now. Cambridge had released her and she was staying in an apartment by herself in the town next to Dover. I wanted to help her and now my dream to do just that was about to materialize.

I went back to bed, hopeful for my future at long last.

Epilogue

I ended up working for DTC for thirteen years and, during that same time, I managed to obtain an MBA from NYU. This time, the company paid for my degree. Right before leaving the company I met a wonderful person who started new in my department. He wasn't new to the company, however. He had started working at DTC around the same time I did. It was strange that we had never really known each other before our meeting. We dated for a few years and in 1999, we became Mr. and Mrs. Mauro. We moved to Texas in 2001 with the idea of starting a family. We now have two wonderful children.

My mother never quite recovered from her downward spiral. Even though she had been released from a mental health facility, it still didn't address her drinking problems. With both kids and her second husband no longer at home, she felt the twinge of loneliness more so than ever and began to drink even harder.

Back in New York, I knew her drinking was spiraling out of control. I tried in vain to help her but later realized it wasn't money that was going to help her. She herself had to be the one to save her now. And that person hadn't arrived yet.

My sister was forced to leave school for the same financial reasons I struggled with year after year. She moved to Texas and later married. Her husband and two children live less than an hour's drive from us. The bond between us has grown even stronger as we continue through life's struggles with each other's help.

I continued meeting with Dad and Shirley year after year. We got to know each other again and every once in a while we exchange pieces of information that continue to fill in the puzzle known as my past. I feel blessed that my sister made that courageous step to reunite with my dad years ago.

As for me, I feel like I finally escaped that past, never to relive it again. I only hope I can now provide my children with the things I had only hoped for and dreamt about when I was little. Funny thing is, I never really dreamt of money so much as I dreamt of love and family. That is what I intend to give my family. May this book be a lesson to them to never take things for granted. Most importantly, I ask that they remember that with God, all things are possible. I prepared this book for them with all my love.

About the Author

Stefanie Straub Photography

Patricia Miller Mauro worked in New York City's financial district for thirteen years. At that time, she obtained an MBA from New York University. She and her husband then moved to Dallas, Texas in 2001 where they are now raising their two children.

During her time in NYC, Patricia wrote the article "A Tribute to My Mother," which was published in the *Recovery Journal* in 1999. Her book is a continuation of that tribute and serves to spread the message to those in similar situations that good news is on its way to those considering a higher education but who are afraid to dream.

McLEAN MERCER REGIONAL LIBRARY
BOX 505
RIVERDALE, ND 58565